P O C K E T S

INSECTS

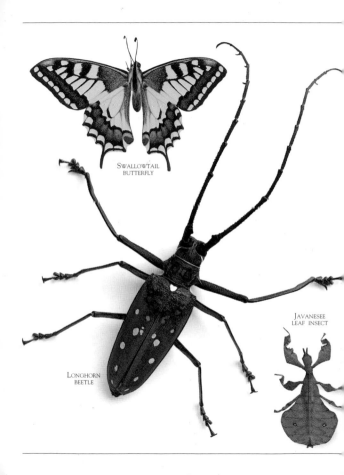

SWALLOWTAIL
BUTTERFLY

JAVANESEE
LEAF INSECT

LONGHORN
BEETLE

P O C K E T S
INSECTS

Written by
LAURENCE MOUND
and STEPHEN BROOKS

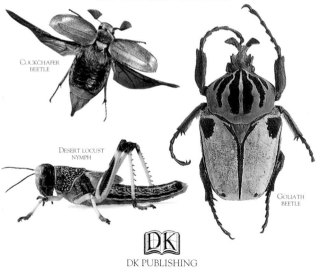

COCKCHAFER
BEETLE

DESERT LOCUST
NYMPH

GOLIATH
BEETLE

DK
DK PUBLISHING

LONDON, NEW YORK,
MELBOURNE, MUNICH, and DELHI

Editor Bernadette Crowley
Art editor Ann Cannings
Senior editor Susan McKeever
Senior art editor Helen Senior
Picture research Caroline Brooke
Production Louise Barratt
US editor Jill Hamilton
US consultant Eric Quinter

REVISED EDITION
Project editor Steve Setford
Designer Sarah Crouch
Managing editor Linda Esposito
Managing art editor Jane Thomas
DTP designer Siu Yin Ho
Consultant Dr George C. McGavin
Production Erica Rosen
US editors Margaret Parrish, Christine Heilman

018-PD044-July/2003

Second American Edition, 2003
Published in the United States by
DK Publishing, Inc., 375 Hudson Street,
New York, New York 10014

11 12 13 14 15 14 13 12 11

Copyright © 2003 Dorling Kindersley Limited

A Cataloging-in-Publication record for the First American Edition of this book
is available from the Library of Congress.

ISBN-13: 978-0-7894-9594-5

Color reproduction by Colourscan, Singapore
Printed in China
See our complete product line at
www.dk.com

CONTENTS

HOW TO USE THIS BOOK

These pages show you how to use *Pockets: Insects*.
The book is divided into several sections. The main
section consists of information on insects from
different habitats. There is also an introductory
section at the front, and a reference section at the
back. Each new section begins
with a picture page.

HABITATS
The insects are arranged into
habitats. In each habitat section
you will find information on the
habitat, and examples of the types
of insects that live there and how
they adapt to their environment.

Running head *Label*

*Corner
coding*

Heading

Introduction

TEMPERATE WOODLAND

ABOUT THE HABITAT
TEMPERATE WOODLANDS are often
dominated by one tree species,
such as oak, which is
deciduous (the trees lose
their leaves in winter).
The types of insect found,
and their numbers, will vary
with the seasons, as well
as with the types of tree
species in the woodlands.

DRAINING
Forests in
wetlands have
many different plant
species. Not people often
drain this habitat because
it is good for farming.
Draining kills plants such
as milk-parsley, the only
plant the English
swallowtail butterfly
will feed on. This
beautiful insect is
now rarely seen.

*Although the
English swallowtail will
lay eggs only on milk-parsley,
adults eat a variety of flowers.*

Size indicator

CORNER CODING
Corners of the pages
are color coded
to remind you
which habitat
section you are in.

- ■ TEMPERATE
  WOODLAND
- ■ GRASSLANDS AND
  HEATHLANDS
- ■ LAKES AND RIVERS
- ■ TROPICAL FOREST
- ■ DESERTS, CAVES,
  AND SOIL
- ■ TOWNS AND
  GARDENS

HEADING
This describes the
subject of the page.
This page is about the
temperate woodland
habitat. If a subject
continues over several
pages, the same
heading applies.

INTRODUCTION
This provides a clear,
general overview of the
subject. After reading
this, you should have
an idea what the pages
are about.

CAPTIONS
AND ANNOTATIONS
Each illustration has a
caption. Annotations, in
italics, point out features of
an illustration and usually
have leader lines.

RUNNING HEADS

These remind you which section you are in. The left-hand page gives the section name. The right-hand page gives the subject. This page, About the Habitat, is in the Temperate Woodland section.

FACT BOXES

Many pages have fact boxes. These contain at-a-glance information about the subject. This fact box gives details such as how many insect species live in oak trees.

SIZE INDICATORS

Some insect pictures have a magnifying glass with a plus (+) or minus (–) sign and a number. This shows how many times bigger (+) or smaller (–) the picture is from life size.

Fact box   *Annotation*

Flowers
Woodlands contain many types of flower. These attract various species of insect, such as bumble bees, which nest in the ground and pollinate many woodland flowers.

VAPOURER MOTH CATERPILLAR
This attractive caterpillar eats the leaves of many different trees in Europe and North America. It will also attack rosebushes and heather plants.

PROCESSIONARY
Conifer forests have fewer types of plant and animal than deciduous forests, although some, such as processionary moth caterpillars, are common. These are named for their habit of following each other head to tail.

Caption

LABELS

For extra clarity, some pictures are accompanied by labels. These may provide extra information, or identify a picture when it is not immediately obvious what it is from the text.

REFERENCE SECTION

The reference section pages are yellow and appear at the back of the book. On these, you will find useful facts, figures, and charts. These pages show the classification of insects and how they fit into the animal kingdom

INDEX

Their are two indexes at the back of the book – a subject index and a latin name index. The subject index lists every subject alphabetically. The latin name index lists the latin name of all the insects in the book.

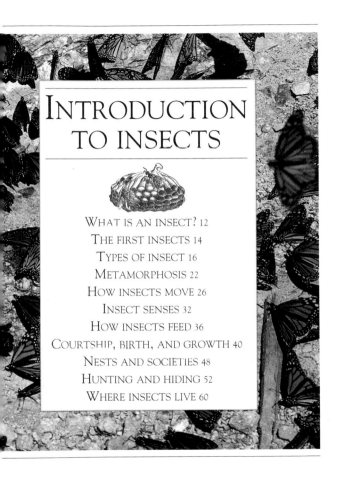

INTRODUCTION
TO INSECTS

WHAT IS AN INSECT?

ABOUT ONE MILLION insect species are known – they are the most abundant animals on Earth. All insects have six legs, and their skeleton is on the outside of their body. This outer skeleton forms a hard, protective armor around the soft internal organs.

DISSECTED BEETLE

The antennae of insects can sense smells and vibrations in the air.

Eye

First part of thorax bears the front legs.

Jointed front leg

SHEDDING SKIN
An immature insect is called a nymph. As each nymph feeds and grows, it must shed its hard outer skin, which is also called an exoskeleton. When it grows too big for its skin, the skin splits, revealing a new, larger skin underneath.

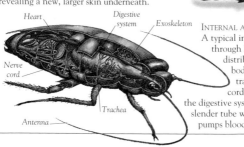

Heart

Digestive system

Exoskeleton

Nerve cord

Trachea

Antenna

INTERNAL ANATOMY
A typical insect breathes through holes in its sides and distributes air around the body in tubes called tracheae. It has a nerve cord which runs beneath the digestive system. The heart, a slender tube with several holes, pumps blood around the body.

The wings are worked by powerful muscles in the thorax.

Claw for gripping surfaces

This end part of an insect's leg is called the tarsus, and is the insect's foot.

...ond and ...d part of ...horax

Hind wing is jointed so it can fold under wing case

Joint where wing folds

— Abdomen

The front wings of beetles are modified into hard wing cases, called elytra, which protect the body.

FLOUR BEETLE LARVA

INSECT FACTS

• Insects belong to the arthropod group, which contains animals with an outer skeleton, such as crabs and spiders.

• They see a wide range of light, from infrared to ultraviolet.

• The small size of insects allows them to breed rapidly.

SOFT BODIES
Larvae such as maggots and caterpillars may feel soft, but they have an exoskeleton like other insects. And like all insect larvae, their skin cannot stretch. It must be shed and grown again as the body gets bigger.

EXTERNAL ANATOMY
Each insect's body has three parts. The head, which bears the eyes, jaws, and antennae; the thorax, which has three sections and bears the legs and wings; and the abdomen, which contains the digestive and reproductive systems.

THE FIRST INSECTS

INSECTS WERE the first animals to appear on land, and also the first to fly. They evolved at least 400 million years ago – long before humans, and even before dinosaurs. Fossils show that some ancient species were similar to modern dragonflies and cockroaches.

INSECT IN AMBER
Amber is fossilized tree resin from pine trees that grew over 40 million years ago. Well-preserved ancient insects are sometimes found in amber. This sweat bee is in fossilized copal, a resin from certain tropical trees.

FLOWER FOOD
When flowering plants evolved 100 million years ago, insects gained two important new foods – pollen and nectar. Insects thrived on these foods. They pollinated the flowers, and many new species of plants and insects evolved together.

FIRST INSECT FACTS

• The ancestors of insects – and all other animals alive on Earth today – were wormlike marine creatures.

• Some of the earliest insects seem to have had three pairs of wings.

• The oldest known butterfly or moth is known from England 190 million years ago.

MODERN EARWIG

Fossil earwig

ROCK REMAINS
This fossil of an earwig was found in 35-million-year-old lake sediment in Colorado. The fossil shows how similar in shape ancient earwigs were to modern ones.

FOSSIL DRAGONFLY

Dragonflies were one of the first types of insect. Fossils show that they have not changed very much in appearance over millions of years. Some ancient dragonflies were very large and may have had wing-spans of over 2 ft (60 cm). This dragonfly fossil, found in southern England, is of a small species. The intricate wing veins can be seen clearly.

Wing laced with veins

End of abdomen

Large eye

Wing veins

MODERN DRAGONFLY

One of the largest present-day dragonflies is this species from Borneo, with a wingspan of 6¼ in (16 cm). Although the nymphs (young) of modern dragonflies live in water, we cannot be sure that this was true of prehistoric dragonflies.

AGILE FLIERS

Modern dragonflies are fast, agile fliers, and ancient dragonflies were probably the same. A prehistoric flying reptile would have had greater trouble catching a dragonfly than this fanciful engraving suggests.

TYPES OF INSECT

SCIENTISTS ARE CONSTANTLY DISCOVERING new insect
They currently know of about one million species, bu
it is likely that there may be at least five million in
total. Each belongs to one of about 30 groups, or
orders, which are defined according to body structure
and larval development.

Beetles, wasps, bees, and ants

About 350,000 species of beetles are
described – they are the largest
order of insects. Wasps, bees,
and ants form the second largest
order of insects, made up of about
125,000 species. The common feature
in this order is a narrow "waist."

Jaws

STAG
BEETLE

*Hard win
cases mee
midline*

*Fringed legs
make swimming
easier.*

GREAT
DIVING
BEETLE

BEETLES

WINGS AND JAWS
The front pair of wings in beetles is
hardened and forms a strong shield ov
the folded hind wings. Some beetles,
such as stag beetles, have greatly
enlarged jaws that look like horns.

DIFFERENT FOODS
Plants, fungi, insects, and dead animals are
among the wide variety of beetle foods. The
great diving beetle lives in ponds. It is a fierce
predator which hunts tadpoles and small fish.

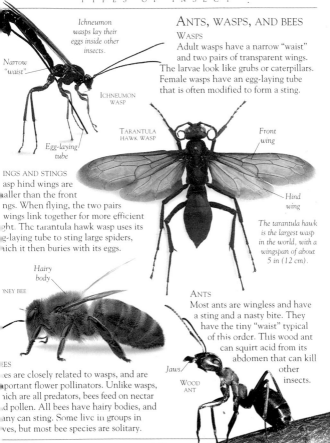

Ichneumon wasps lay their eggs inside other insects.

Narrow "waist"

ICHNEUMON WASP

Egg-laying tube

ANTS, WASPS, AND BEES

WASPS

Adult wasps have a narrow "waist" and two pairs of transparent wings. The larvae look like grubs or caterpillars. Female wasps have an egg-laying tube that is often modified to form a sting.

TARANTULA HAWK WASP

Front wing

Hind wing

The tarantula hawk is the largest wasp in the world, with a wingspan of about 5 in (12 cm).

WINGS AND STINGS

Wasp hind wings are smaller than the front wings. When flying, the two pairs of wings link together for more efficient flight. The tarantula hawk wasp uses its egg-laying tube to sting large spiders, which it then buries with its eggs.

Hairy body

HONEY BEE

BEES

Bees are closely related to wasps, and are important flower pollinators. Unlike wasps, which are all predators, bees feed on nectar and pollen. All bees have hairy bodies, and many can sting. Some live in groups in hives, but most bee species are solitary.

ANTS

Most ants are wingless and have a sting and a nasty bite. They have the tiny "waist" typical of this order. This wood ant can squirt acid from its abdomen that can kill other insects.

Jaws

WOOD ANT

Butterflies, moths, and flies

Two common insect orders are the two-winged flies and the moths and butterflies. Flies are distinctive because their second pair of wings is converted into balancing organs that resemble drumsticks. Their young stages are maggots. Butterflies and moths have a coiled proboscis (feeding tube), and their wings are covered in minute, flattened scales. Butterfly and moth larvae are called caterpillars.

BUTTERFLIES AND MOTHS

CATERPILLARS

Although caterpillars' bodies are soft, they have an exoskeleton like other insects. Caterpillars grow at a very fast rate. They feed on leaves and have sharp jaws for slicing vegetation.

Leaf-green coloring

Feathery antenna

MOTHS

There are 150,000 species of moth. Most moth species fly only at night. They are usually dull in color and they often have feathery antennae. There are also many day-flying species, and some of these are brightly colored.

POLYPHEMUS
MOTH

BUTTERFLIES

There are 15,000 species of butterfly. Most butterflies fly by day, have club-tipped antennae, and are brightly colored. The scales that cover moths and butterflies sometimes produce colors by iridescence, which is the effect of sunlight shining on them to produce a display of many different colors.

Club-tipped antenna

SWALLOWTAIL
BUTTERFLY

FLIES

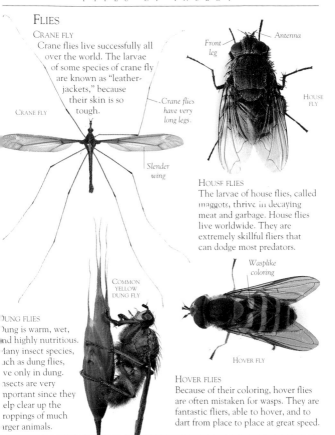

CRANE FLY
Crane flies live successfully all over the world. The larvae of some species of crane fly are known as "leather-jackets," because their skin is so tough.

CRANE FLY

Crane flies have very long legs.

Slender wing

Front leg

Antenna

HOUSE FLY

HOUSE FLIES
The larvae of house flies, called maggots, thrive in decaying meat and garbage. House flies live worldwide. They are extremely skillful fliers that can dodge most predators.

Wasplike coloring

COMMON YELLOW DUNG FLY

DUNG FLIES
Dung is warm, wet, and highly nutritious. Many insect species, such as dung flies, live only in dung. Insects are very important since they help clear up the droppings of much larger animals.

HOVER FLY

HOVER FLIES
Because of their coloring, hover flies are often mistaken for wasps. They are fantastic fliers, able to hover, and to dart from place to place at great speed.

Bugs and other types

There are about 67,500 species of bug, the fifth-largest order of insects. Bugs have a feeding tube folded back between the legs, and most of them eat plant food. The other orders of insects contain fewer species. Some of these orders are well known, such as fleas, cockroaches, dragonflies, and locusts.

BUGS

FEEDING TUBES

The mandibles (jaws) found in most insects are modified in bugs into a needlelike tube called a rostrum. The bug pierces food with its rostrum and then sucks up juices.

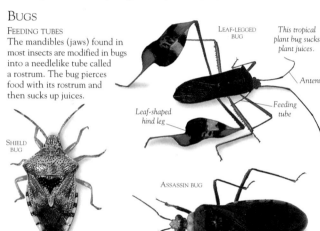

LEAF-LEGGED BUG

This tropical plant bug sucks plant juices.

Antenna

Feeding tube

Leaf-shaped hind leg

SHIELD BUG

ASSASSIN BUG

SHIELD BUGS

Bugs have two pairs of wings. The front wings are quite hard, although not as hard as those of beetles. Shield bugs are so called because when their wings are closed, they look like colorful shields.

ASSASSIN BUGS

Not all bugs feed on plants. Assassin bugs feed on other insects. They stab prey with their feeding tube and then suck out the victim's juices. Some South American assassin bugs feed on the blood of humans and transmit diseases.

Wing buds

DESERT LOCUST NYMPH

OTHER INSECT ORDERS

GRASSHOPPERS

The desert locust belongs to the order that includes crickets and grasshoppers. These insects eat plants and have powerful back legs for leaping.

MANTID

MANTIDS

Adults and mantid nymphs look very similar. They both have very large eyes and grasping front legs. Many mantids are colored like leaves or flowers, so they can hide in them as they wait for their prey to come near.

STICK INSECT

COCKROACH

COCKROACHES

There are many fossils of cockroaches, since they are one of the most ancient orders of insects. Their front wings overlap each other, instead of meeting in the middle, and the young stages look like the adults.

DRAGONFLY

STICK INSECTS

This order is usually found in the tropics. They look like sticks with their long, slender legs and bodies and feed only on leaves. Their sticklike disguise hides them from predators.

Wings have many veins.

DRAGONFLIES

The ancestors of dragonflies and damselflies appeared at least 300 million years ago. The nymphs of these insects live in water. Like the adults, which catch their prey in flight, they are predators.

METAMORPHOSIS

INSECTS GO THROUGH several stages of growth before
they become adults. This growing process is called
metamorphosis. There are two types of metamorphosis,
complete and incomplete. Complete metamorphosis
has four growth stages – egg, larva, pupa, and adult.
Incomplete metamorphosis involves three stages – egg,
nymph, and adult.

Incomplete metamorphosis

This growing process is a
gradual transformation. The
insects hatch from their
eggs looking like miniature
adults. These young insects
are called nymphs. As they
grow, they shed their skin
several times before they
reach the adult stage.

Adult head

Adult head and thorax emerge

Clawed feet hook onto stem.

Wing buds

1 DAMSELFLY NYMPH
A damselfly nymph
lives underwater. Paddle-
like plates on its tail help it
swim and breathe. It sheds
its skin several times as it
grows toward adulthood.

2 HOLDING ON
When the nymph is
ready to change into an
adult it crawls out of the
water up a plant stem.

3 BREAKING OUT
The skin along the
back splits open and
the adult head and
thorax start to emerge.

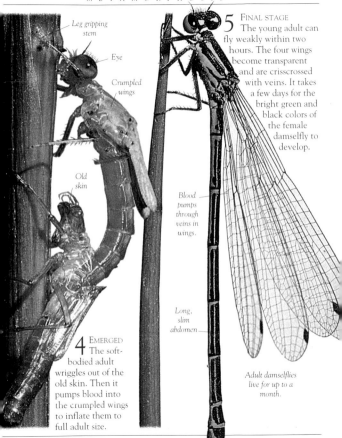

Leg gripping stem

Eye

Crumpled wings

Old skin

5 FINAL STAGE
The young adult can fly weakly within two hours. The four wings become transparent and are crisscrossed with veins. It takes a few days for the bright green and black colors of the female damselfly to develop.

Blood pumps through veins in wings.

Long, slim abdomen

4 EMERGED
The soft-bodied adult wriggles out of the old skin. Then it pumps blood into the crumpled wings to inflate them to full adult size.

Adult damselflies live for up to a month.

Complete metamorphosis

The four growth stages in a complete metamorphosis are egg, larva, pupa, and adult. The larva bears no resemblance to the adult it will become. During the pupa stage the larva makes the amazing transformation into an adult. Insects such as wasps, butterflies, beetles, and flies undergo complete metamorphosis.

1 LAYING EGGS
Butterflies lay eggs near leaves that caterpillars can eat when they hatch. Newly hatched caterpillars are too small to walk far to feed.

Egg

2 THE FIRST MEAL
When a caterpillar emerges, the first meal it eats is usually its own eggshell. The eggshell provides the caterpillar with valuable nutrients before it begins its diet of leaves.

Eggshell

Strong jaws slice food.

A caterpillar can increase its body weight by about 100 times in a few weeks.

3 GROWING
The caterpillar chews up leaves and grows much bigger, shedding its skin several times. This growth prepares the caterpillar for the pupal stage of its life.

A butterfly pupa is also known as a chrysalis.

Silk thread holds pupa in place.

A butterfly pupa often looks like a leaf for camouflage.

4 PUPA ACTIVITY
A pupa is like a busy factory. From the outside it looks still, but inside there is a great deal of activity. The caterpillar's organs turn into a milky liquid, and new butterfly organs grow rapidly in their place.

5 CHANGE COMPLETED
Once the metamorphosis is complete, the butterfly emerges from its pupa. It stretches its wet, crumpled wings. Before the butterfly is ready to fly, it must wait a couple of hours for its wings to expand and harden.

Antenna

Wet, crumpled wings

Empty pupa

Blood is pumped into the veins in the wings to expand them.

SWALLOWTAIL BUTTERFLY

takes about eight weeks for this swallowtail butterfly to grow from egg to adult.

6 BUTTERFLY
The fully developed butterfly leads a totally different life from the caterpillar. While caterpillars eat leaves in order to grow, butterflies spend their time sipping nectar from flowers and seeking a mate.

HOW INSECTS MOVE

INSECTS MOVE using muscles which are attached
to the inner surfaces of their hard outer skeleton.
Many insects walk, but some larvae have no legs so
they crawl or wriggle along. Some insects swim,
others jump, but most adult insects can fly and in
this way they may travel long distances.

Legs

Insects use their legs for walking,
running, jumping, and swimming.
Many insects have legs modified
for a number of other purposes.
These include catching prey,
holding a female when mating,
producing songs, digging, fighting,
and camouflage.

LEGS FOR SWIMMING
The backswimmer has long, oar-
shaped back legs, allowing the insect
to "row" rapidly through water. The
legs have flattened ends and a fringe
of thick hairs. The front legs are short
to grasp prey on the water's surface.

MOVEMENT FACTS

• Fairyflies use
their wings to "fly"
underwater.

• Many butterflies walk
on four legs; the front
pair are used for tasting.

• The legless larvae of
some parasitic wasps
hitch a ride on a
passing ant in order to
enter an ant's nest.

---

1 PREPARING TO JUMP
The back legs of locusts are swollen and packed
with strong muscles for jumping. Before leaping, a
locust holds its back legs tightly under its body, near its
center of gravity. This is the best position for the legs
to propel the insect
high into the air.

Long back
legs

Wing

Shorter
front legs

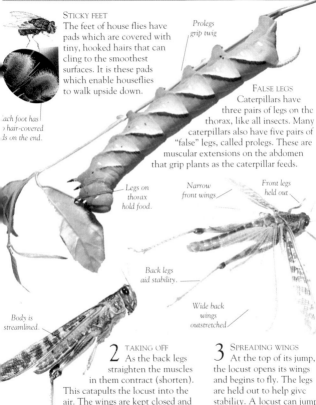

STICKY FEET
The feet of house flies have pads which are covered with tiny, hooked hairs that can cling to the smoothest surfaces. It is these pads which enable houseflies to walk upside down.

Each foot has hair-covered ds on the end.

Prolegs grip twig

FALSE LEGS
Caterpillars have three pairs of legs on the thorax, like all insects. Many caterpillars also have five pairs of "false" legs, called prolegs. These are muscular extensions on the abdomen that grip plants as the caterpillar feeds.

Legs on thorax hold food.

Narrow front wings

Front legs held out

Back legs aid stability.

Wide back wings outstretched

Body is streamlined.

2 TAKING OFF
As the back legs straighten the muscles in them contract (shorten). This catapults the locust into the air. The wings are kept closed and the front legs tucked under the body, so the insect is streamlined.

3 SPREADING WINGS
At the top of its jump, the locust opens its wings and begins to fly. The legs are held out to help give stability. A locust can jump about 19½ in (50 cm) – 10 times its own body length.

Wings and scales

Insect wings are a wide variety of shapes and sizes. They are used not just for flying but also for attracting a mate or hiding from predators. Most insects have two pairs of wings, each with a network of veins to give strength. Flies have only one pair of wings – the second pair is modified into small balancing organs called halteres. Small insects have few wing veins since their wings are so tiny.

EXPERT FLIERS

Dragonflies are among the most accomplished fliers in the insect world. They can hover, fly fast or slow, change direction rapidly, and even fly backward. As they maneuver, their two pairs of wings beat independently of each other.

Long antenna

Large front wing

The hind wings are about 2½ in (6.5 cm) long.

WING FACTS

• The scales of butterflies and moths contain waste products from the pupal stage.

• There is a hearing organ in one of the wing veins of green lacewings for hearing the shrieks of bats.

• Scientists still have a lot to learn about how insects fly and control their flight once airborne.

LACEWINGS

The hind wings of ribbon-tail lacewings are modified into long graceful streamers. Scientists are not sure what these are for, but they may act as stabilizers in flight, or even divert predators from attacking the lacewing's body. The lacewing's mottled patterns probably help to conceal it in the dry, sandy places where it lives.

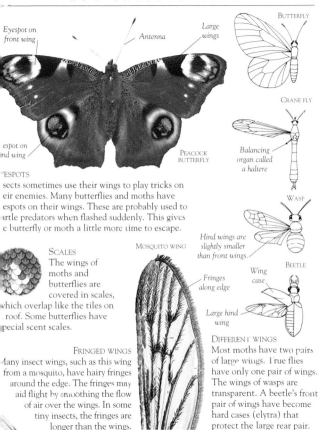

Eyespot on front wing

Antenna

Large wings

BUTTERFLY

espot on nd wing

PEACOCK BUTTERFLY

CRANE FLY

Balancing organ called a haltere

WASP

Hind wings are slightly smaller than front wings

'YESPOTS

sects sometimes use their wings to play tricks on eir enemies. Many butterflies and moths have espots on their wings. These are probably used to artle predators when flashed suddenly. This gives e butterfly or moth a little more time to escape.

SCALES

The wings of moths and butterflies are covered in scales, which overlap like the tiles on roof. Some butterflies have pecial scent scales.

MOSQUITO WING

FRINGED WINGS

Many insect wings, such as this wing from a mosquito, have hairy fringes around the edge. The fringes may aid flight by smoothing the flow of air over the wings. In some tiny insects, the fringes are longer than the wings.

Fringes along edge

BEETLE

Wing case

Large hind wing

DIFFERENT WINGS

Most moths have two pairs of large wings. True flies have only one pair of wings. The wings of wasps are transparent. A beetle's front pair of wings have become hard cases (elytra) that protect the large rear pair.

Flight

The ability to fly is one of the main reasons insects have survived for millions of years, and continue to flourish. Flight helps insects escape from danger. It also makes it easier to find food and new places to live. Sometimes insects fly thousands of miles to reach fresh food or warmer weather.

WARMING UP
An insect's flight muscles must be warm before the wings can be moved fast enough for flight. On cool mornings, insects such as bumblebees have to vibrate their wings to warm themselves up.

FLYING GROUPS
This African grasshopper has broad hind wings whic allow it to glide for long distances. Locusts are a ty of grasshopper that fly in huge groups when they need new food.
Sometimes as many as 1 million locusts fly togethe for hundreds of miles.

1 PREPARING TO FLY
This cockchafer beetle prepares for flight by climbing to the top of a plant and facing into the wind. It may open and shut its elytra (wing cases) several times while warming up.

Elytra protect body.

2 OPENING THE WINGS
The hardened elytra, which protect the fragile hind wings, begi to open. Th antennae ar spread so the beetle can monitor the wind direction

30

ACROBATS OF THE AIR
Hoverflies are capable of incredible
acrobatics in the air. They can move like a
helicopter – forward, backward, sideways,
and directly upward or downward. They can
also hover, a flight maneuver that very few
insects are capable of.

*Wings are fully
open and have
begun to beat.*

*Elytra held
out to
provide lift*

*Leading
edge of
wing*

*Outstretched legs
help stabilize
beetle as it steers
through the air.*

*Antenna can
sense air
movements.*

*Wings
have a
joint which
unfolds.*

4 IN FLIGHT
The cockchafer leaps into the
air, legs outstretched to aid stability.
The hind wings are beating, driving
the insect forward. On the upbeat, the
leading edge of the wing is
pulled upward and backward. On
the downbeat it travels downward
and forward.

3 ALMOST OFF
The elytra are
opened wide and the
hind wings rapidly
unfold. The hind
wings provide propulsion
during flight, and the elytra
assist by providing lift, like the
wings of an airplane.

INSECT SENSES

INSECTS NEED to be fully aware of the world around them in order to survive. Although insects are tiny, some have keener senses than many larger animals. They can see colors and hear sounds that are undetectable to humans, as well as being able to detect smells from many miles away.

Sight

HEAD OF COMMON
DARTER DRAGONFLY

There are two types of insect eyes – simple and compound. Simple eyes can probably detect only light and shade. Compound eyes have hundreds of lenses, giving their owner excellent vision.

SIMPLE EYES
Caterpillars never need to look far for their plant food – they are constantly surrounded by it. Because of this, they do not need sharp eyesight. They can manage perfectly well with a group of simple eyes.

GOOD VISION
The eyes of dragonflies take up most of their head. This allows them to see what's in front, above, below, and behind them all at the same time. Dragonflies use their excellent sight and agile flight to catch prey.

Simple
eyes

COMMON DARTER
DRAGONFLY

EYE CONSTRUCTION
Compound eyes are made up of many individual facets, called ommatidia. Each ommatidium has a lens at the top, with a second, conical-shaped lens underneath. The more ommatidia there are, the more sensitive is the eye.

Lens at top of ommatidium

Conical lens

Three simple eyes

Compound eye

ULTRAVIOLET LIGHT
Insects can see ultraviolet light, which humans and most other animals cannot see. The petals of some flowers have lines called honey guides which reflect ultraviolet light, and direct insects to the flower's store of pollen and nectar.

The wasp's simple eyes are called ocelli.

Antenna

Carnivorous insects like this wasp have excellent vision for catching prey.

LOTS OF EYES
Like most insects, this wasp has both compound and simple eyes. We do not know what kind of view of the world compound eyes give insects. It is thought that each ommatidium gives a different image, building up a mosaic-like picture. We do know that compound eyes can detect the slightest movement, and can see certain colors.

Jaws

Smelling, hearing, and touching

The bodies of insects are covered in short hairs which are connected to the nervous system. These hairs can feel, or "hear," vibrations in the air due to either sound or movement. Some ha are modified to detect smells and flavors. Sensory hairs are ofter found on the antennae, but also occur on the feet and mouthpa

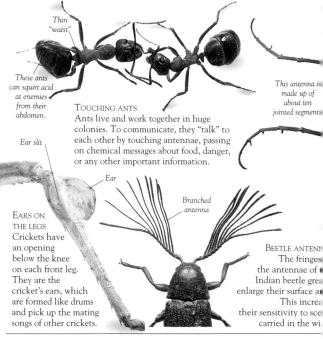

Thin "waist"

These ants can squirt acid at enemies from their abdomen.

This antenna is made up of about ten jointed segments

TOUCHING ANTS
Ants live and work together in huge colonies. To communicate, they "talk" to each other by touching antennae, passing on chemical messages about food, danger, or any other important information.

Ear slit

Ear

Branched antenna

EARS ON THE LEGS
Crickets have an opening below the knee on each front leg. They are the cricket's ears, which are formed like drums and pick up the mating songs of other crickets.

BEETLE ANTENN
The fringes the antennae of Indian beetle grea enlarge their surface a This increas their sensitivity to sce carried in the wi

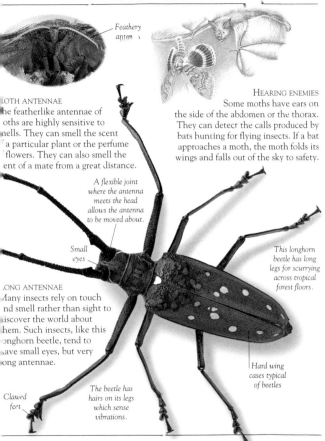

Feathery antenna

MOTH ANTENNAE

The featherlike antennae of moths are highly sensitive to smells. They can smell the scent of a particular plant or the perfume of flowers. They can also smell the scent of a mate from a great distance.

HEARING ENEMIES

Some moths have ears on the side of the abdomen or the thorax. They can detect the calls produced by bats hunting for flying insects. If a bat approaches a moth, the moth folds its wings and falls out of the sky to safety.

A flexible joint where the antenna meets the head allows the antenna to be moved about.

Small eyes

This longhorn beetle has long legs for scurrying across tropical forest floors.

LONG ANTENNAE

Many insects rely on touch and smell rather than sight to discover the world about them. Such insects, like this longhorn beetle, tend to have small eyes, but very long antennae.

Hard wing cases typical of beetles

Clawed feet

The beetle has hairs on its legs which sense vibrations.

HOW INSECTS FEED

INSECTS HAVE complex mouthpart. The insects that chew their food have a pair of strong jaws for chopping, a smaller pair of jaws for holding food, and two pairs of sensory organs, called palps, for tasting. Some insects drink only liquid food and have special tubular mouthparts like a straw.

Jaws chew leaf.

Caterpillar holds leaf with its legs.

Chewing

Predatory, chewing insects need sharp, pointed jaws for stabbing, holding, and chopping up their struggling prey. Insects that chew plants have blunter jaws for grinding their food.

PLANT CHEWER
A caterpillar needs powerful jaws to bite into plant material. Their jaws are armed with teeth that overlap when they close. Some caterpillars' jaws are modified into grinding plates for mashing up the toughest leaves.

THRUSTING JAWS
Dragonfly larvae have pincers at the end of a hinged plate folded under the head. When catching prey, the plate unfolds, shoots forward, and the pincers grab the prey. Toothed jaws in the head reduce the victim to mincemeat.

3 6

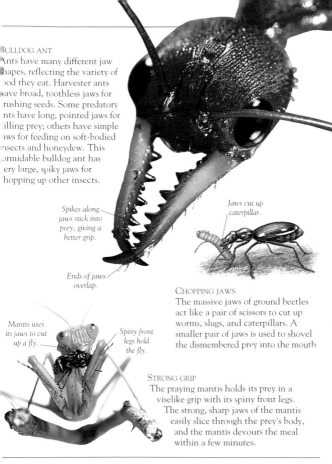

BULLDOG ANT

Ants have many different jaw shapes, reflecting the variety of food they eat. Harvester ants have broad, toothless jaws for crushing seeds. Some predatory ants have long, pointed jaws for killing prey; others have simple jaws for feeding on soft-bodied insects and honeydew. This formidable bulldog ant has very large, spiky jaws for chopping up other insects.

Spikes along jaws stick into prey, giving a better grip.

Jaws cut up caterpillar.

Ends of jaws overlap.

CHOPPING JAWS

The massive jaws of ground beetles act like a pair of scissors to cut up worms, slugs, and caterpillars. A smaller pair of jaws is used to shovel the dismembered prey into the mouth

Mantis uses its jaws to cut up a fly.

Spiny front legs hold the fly.

STRONG GRIP

The praying mantis holds its prey in a viselike grip with its spiny front legs. The strong, sharp jaws of the mantis easily slice through the prey's body, and the mantis devours the meal within a few minutes.

Drinking

For many insects, the main way of feeding is by drinking. The most nutritious foods to drink are nectar and blood. Nectar is rich in sugar, and blood is packed with proteins. Some insects drink by sucking through strawlike mouthparts. Others have spongelike mouthparts with which they mop up liquids.

HAWK MOTH
Butterflies and moths have a long, tonguelike tube called a proboscis through which they drink. Darwin's hawk moth has an extremely long proboscis for reaching the nectar in an extra-long flower.

Moth hovers in front of flower.

Proboscis

Nectar far back in flower

The hairs are sensitive to touch, taste, and air movement.

Houseflies have taste buds on their feet.

HOUSEFLY

MOPPING MOUT
Houseflies have a spong
pad to mop up liquid
Their saliva contain
juices which tur
solid food into
mushy liquid. Stabl
flies are similar t
houseflies, but they drin
blood. Their feeding pa
has teeth which cut a
animal's skin t
make it bleed

Spongy mouthpart

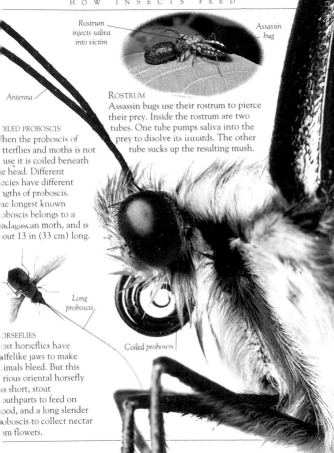

ROSTRUM
Assassin bugs use their rostrum to pierce
their prey. Inside the rostrum are two
tubes. One tube pumps saliva into the
prey to disolve its innards. The other
tube sucks up the resulting mush.

*Rostrum
injects saliva
into victim*

*Assassin
bug*

Antenna

OILED PROBOSCIS
hen the proboscis of
tterflies and moths is not
use it is coiled beneath
e head. Different
ecies have different
gths of proboscis.
e longest known
oboscis belongs to a
adagascan moth, and is
out 13 in (33 cm) long.

*Long
proboscis*

ORSEFLIES
ost horseflies have
lfelike jaws to make
imals bleed. But this
rious oriental horsefly
s short, stout
outhparts to feed on
ood, and a long slender
oboscis to collect nectar
m flowers.

Coiled proboscis

COURTSHIP, BIRTH, AND GROWTH

REPRODUCTION is hazardous for insects. A female must first mate with a male of her own species and lay eggs where the newly hatched young can feed. The larvae must shed their skin several times as they grow. All this time the insects must avoid being eaten.

Courtship and mating

Males and females use special signals to ensure that their chosen mate is the right species. Courtship usually involves using scents, but may include color displays, dancing, caressing, and even gifts.

The light is produced by a chemical reaction.

GUIDING LIGHT
Glowworms are the wingless females of certain beetle species. They attract males by producing a light near the tip of their abdomen. Some species flash a distinctive code to attract the correct males.

Butterflies find the scented chemicals, called pheromones, very attractive.

COURTSHIP FLIGHTS
Butterflies may recognize their own species by sight, but scent is more reliable. Butterfly courtship involves dancing flights with an exchange of scented chemical signals specific to each species.

MATING DANGER
Mating between some insect species may last for several hours, with the male gripping the female's abdomen with claspers. This keeps other males away, but the pair are vulnerable to predators at this time.

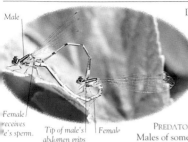

Male

Female receives 'e's sperm.

Tip of male's abdomen grips female.

Female

DAMSELFLIES

When mating, a male damselfly grips a female's neck with the tip of his abdomen. She receives a packet of sperm from a pouch near his legs; he continues to hold her neck while she lays eggs. This prevents other males from mating with her.

PREDATORS MATING

Males of some predatory species, such as empid flies, give the female a meal of a dead insect when mating so they are not eaten themselves. Sometimes the male tricks the female by presenting her with useless, inedible gifts such as seeds.

Female

Female

MATING ASIAN
SWALLOWTAIL
BUTTERFLIES

Male

UNNATURAL BEHAVIOR

It is often said that a female mantis eats the male while he is mating with her. But this probably happens only when the mantises are in captivity and their behavior is not natural.

Eggs and egg-laying

Insects use up a lot of energy producing eggs. To make sure this energy is not wasted, insects have many ways of protecting their eggs from predators. A few species of insect stay with their eggs to protect them until the larvae hatch. Some insects lay their eggs underground with a supply of food waiting for the newly hatched larvae. Most insects lay their eggs either in or near food, so the young larvae do not have to travel far to eat.

The egg-laying tube, also known as an ovipositor, drills into the wood.

The ovipositor is longer than the ichneumon's body.

ICHNEUMON WASP
The larvae of ichneumon wasps are parasites, which means they feed on other living creatures. When finding a host for its egg, an adult ichneumon detects the vibrations of a beetle grub gnawing inside a tree trunk. The wasp drives its egg-laying tube into the trunk until it finds the grub. An egg is laid on the grub, which then provides food for the wasp larva when it hatches.

SUITABLE FOOD

Butterflies desert their eggs once they are laid. Different butterflies lay their eggs on different plants, depending on what the larvae eat. The Malay lacewing butterfly lays its eggs on vine tendrils.

Wasp carrying beetle to nest

Beetles are stored in underground nest.

CARING EARWIGS

A female earwig looks [after] her eggs, licking them regularly to keep them clean. When the nymphs hatch, she feeds them until they [are] big enough to leave the nest.

vertical main tunnel

Earwig eggs

HUNTING WASPS

Most species of hunting wasp collect soft-bodied prey, such as caterpillars or spiders, for their grubs. But the weevil-hunting wasp collects adult beetles, which it stings and then stores in a tunnel as food for its larvae.

Beetles mold dung into balls.

Beetle fills tunnel with dung as food for newly hatched grubs.

INSECT EGG FACTS

• Whitefly eggs have stalks that extract water from leaves.

• Tsetse flies develop their eggs internally and lay mature larvae.

• Green lacewing eggs have long stalks, making them difficult for predators to eat.

DUNG BEETLES

The males and females of some dung beetle species work together to dig an underground tunnel with smaller tunnels branching off it. A female lays an egg in each of the smaller tunnels and fills them with animal dung, which the beetle grubs will feed on.

Birth and growth

Newborn aphid

As an insect grows from egg to adult it sheds its skin several times to produce a larger exoskeleton. While this new skin hardens the insect is soft and vulnerable. Insects have many life-cycle adaptations to protect their soft young stages.

EGGS LARVA PUPA ADULT LADYBUG

LADYBUG GROWTH

Ladybugs and all other beetles go through a complete metamorphosis. An adult ladybug lays its eggs on a plant where small insects called aphids feed. Ladybug larvae eat aphids and shed their skin three times as they grow. The colorful adult emerges from the dull resting stage, or pupa.

APHIDS

Female aphids can reproduce without matin_ They give birth to live young rather than lay egg and each female may hav about 100 offspring. The newborn aphids can give birth after only a few day

FROTHY PROTECTIO

Spittlebugs are soft-bodied bugs lik aphids. A spittlebug nymph produce frothy liquid excrement from i anus. The froth protects th nymph from drying out, an also hides it fro predator

Frothy hideaway

Froth contains a special chemical to make it long-lasting

PARENTAL CARE
The females of some species of shield bug stay with their eggs and young nymphs to protect them. If touched, the parent produces a powerful smell, giving these bugs the alternative name of stinkbugs.

SHIELD BUG NYMPHS WITH PARENT

Hopper burrowing to surface

Eggs

BURROWING NYMPHS
A female locust can extend her abdomen to almost twice its length when laying eggs. The eggs are placed deep in the soil for protection. The newborn nymphs, called hoppers, must burrow to the surface to feed.

Nymph was removed from its froth for this photograph

SPITTLEBUG NYMPH

LEAVING WATER
Unlike all other insects, mayflies have two adult stages. The first stage, the subadult, crawls out of the water where it lived as a nymph. It flies weakly and is dull colored. It soon molts to produce the true adult, which then mates.

Adult mayfly

Subadult emerging from water

Nymph

Survival of the young

Predators eagerly hunt insect larvae since many are slow-moving
soft, and nutritious. To ensure survival, most insect species produ
large numbers of young which grow rapidly. Most insect larvae a
defenseless and have developed special ways of hiding from
predators. But many insect larvae are fierce
predators themselves, consuming other
creatures for nourishment as they grow.

*Grub in
pupal cell*

WELL HIDDEN
The larvae of chafer beetles live
underground, safely hidden from
most predators. The larvae, or
grubs, may take many weeks to
develop. They then produce a
cell of hardened soil in which
they will change into an adult.

*Eyespots make fron
thorax resemb
fearsome*

*Real
head*

*Sharp
spines*

SPINY LARVA
Mexican bean
beetle larvae
eat leaves
and develop
rapidly. They
are covered
with long,
branched spines
which may deter
birds and other
predators from
attacking them.

*True
legs*

Proleg

**SCARY
DISPLAY**
Caterpillars are a
favorite food of birds.
Some caterpillars try to
hide to stay safe. But if the puss
moth caterpillar is threatened, it puts on a
startling display which can frighten off birds.

WATER LARVA
Stonefly larvae live in cold water and grow slowly, spending about three years as a larva. They are slow-moving and hide from predators under rocks and among plants.

NIGHT FEEDER
The mormon butterfly caterpillar feeds in the dark of night to avoid being seen by predators. In less than eight hours it will chew away a leaf which is more than twice its own length. During the day it rests as inconspicuously as possible.

For a more frightening display, the caterpillar waves these "tails" as if they were stings.

SOFT BODIES
Young mantids are fierce predators. The body of some species resembles a flower. This disguise helps them to go unnoticed by prey, and also by predators such as birds.

Eye

Pink, flowerlike body

Leg

Legs are striped pink and green.

NESTS AND SOCIETIES

MOST INSECTS lead solitary lives, but
some, particularly wasps, ants, bees,
and termites, live in societies which
are sometimes very ordered. There
are queens, kings, workers, and
soldiers. Each of these has particular
jobs to do. Social insects live in nests
which are often elaborate, where they
protect each other and rear their young.

TROPICAL WASP NEST
MADE OF CHEWED-UP
PLANT FIBERS

Wasps, ants, and bees

These insects produce a wide range of nests. Some
are small with only a few dozen members, but
larger nests may contain thousands or even
millions of insects. Most have a single queen
and all the nest members are her offspring.

*The nest is
cemented together
with wasp saliva.*

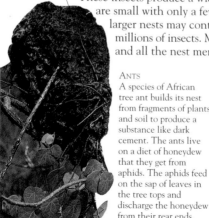

ANTS
A species of African
tree ant builds its nest
from fragments of plants
and soil to produce a
substance like dark
cement. The ants live
on a diet of honeydew
that they get from
aphids. The aphids feed
on the sap of leaves in
the tree tops and
discharge the honeydew
from their rear ends.

BEES
A bumblebee queen starts
her nest alone in spring in
a hole in the ground. She
makes cells for her eggs ou
of wax. She also makes a
wax pot which she fills
with honey for food.

The queen uses her antennae to measure the cells as she builds them.

A NEW START

European wasp colonies die out each winter. In spring a queen begins a new nest of "paper" made with chewed-up wood. She makes new cells for her eggs, building walls around the cells to shield them.

Finished nest

Entrance hole

2 PROTECTIVE LAYERS

The queen builds more and more paper layers around the cells. The layers will protect the larvae from cold winds as well as from predators. The queen leaves an entrance hole at the bottom.

3 HARD-WORKING FAMILY

The first brood the queen rears become workers, gathering food for more larvae and expanding the nest. By summer, a nest may have 500 wasps, all collecting caterpillars for the larvae. A large nest may be as much as 18 in (45 cm) in diameter.

INSIDE THE NEST

The queen lays a single egg in each cell. When the larvae hatch they stay in their cell and the queen feeds them with pieces of chewed-up caterpillar.

Termite nests

Termites have the most complex insect societies. Their elaborate nests, which may be in wood or underground, last for several years. Each nest has a single large queen and king, which are served by specialized small workers and large soldiers. Termites feed and protect each other, and one generation will help raise the next generation of offspring.

QUEEN TERMITE
In a termite society, the queen lays all the eggs. She is too fa move, so the workers bring fo to her. The queen lays 30,000 eggs each day and, as she lays them, the workers carry them to special chambers for rearin

Layers of "umbrellas"

NEST DEFENDERS
Termite soldiers fight enemies th attack the nest. Most termite spec have soldiers with enlarged heads and powerful jaws. In some specie each soldier's head has a snout th squirts poison at invaders.

UMBRELLA NEST
The curved layers on this African termite nest like umbrellas and protect the nest from heavy rain. If an "umbrella" is damaged, it does not ge repaired, but a new one may be built.

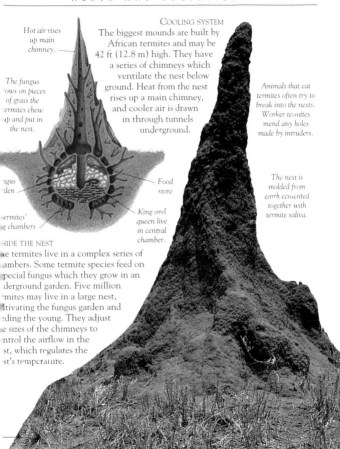

Hot air rises up main chimney.

The fungus grows on pieces of grass the termites chew up and put in the nest.

COOLING SYSTEM
The biggest mounds are built by African termites and may be 42 ft (12.8 m) high. They have a series of chimneys which ventilate the nest below ground. Heat from the nest rises up a main chimney, and cooler air is drawn in through tunnels underground.

Animals that eat termites often try to break into the nests. Worker termites mend any holes made by intruders.

The nest is molded from earth cemented together with termite saliva.

ngus den

Food store

ermites' g chambers

King and queen live in central chamber.

SIDE THE NEST
e termites live in a complex series of ambers. Some termite species feed on pecial fungus which they grow in an derground garden. Five million rmites may live in a large nest, ltivating the fungus garden and eding the young. They adjust e sizes of the chimneys to ntrol the airflow in the st, which regulates the st's temperature.

HUNTING AND HIDING

SOME INSECT SPECIES are deadly hunters, killing prey
with poisonous stings and sharp jaws. Insects are also
hunted by a huge number of animals. To hide from
predators, many insects have developed special
disguises and patterns of behavior.

Hunting insects

About one-third of insect species are
carnivorous (they eat meat). Some species
eat decaying meat and dung, but most
carnivorous insects hunt for their food.

KILLER BEETLE
Some insects are easily
recognized as predators.
The large jaws of this
African ground beetle
indicate that it is a hunt
and its long legs show
that it can run fast
after its insect prey

KILLER WASPS
There are many
types of hunting
wasp. Most adult
hunting wasps are
vegetarians – they
hunt prey only as food
for their larvae. Each
hunting wasp species hu
a particular type of prey.
The weevil-hunting wasp
hunts only a type of beetle
called a weevil.

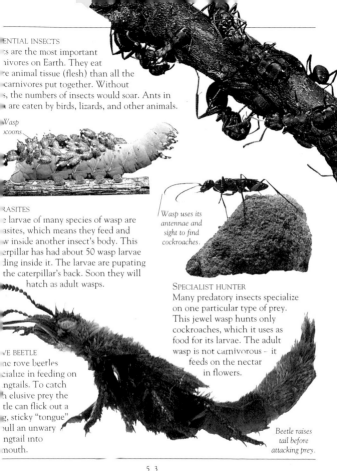

...ENTIAL INSECTS

...s are the most important
...nivores on Earth. They eat
...re animal tissue (flesh) than all the
...carnivores put together. Without
...s, the numbers of insects would soar. Ants in
...a are eaten by birds, lizards, and other animals.

*Wasp
...ocoons*

...RASITES

...e larvae of many species of wasp are
...asites, which means they feed and
...w inside another insect's body. This
...erpillar has had about 50 wasp larvae
...ding inside it. The larvae are pupating
...the caterpillar's back. Soon they will
hatch as adult wasps.

*Wasp uses its
antennae and
sight to find
cockroaches.*

SPECIALIST HUNTER

Many predatory insects specialize
on one particular type of prey.
This jewel wasp hunts only
cockroaches, which it uses as
food for its larvae. The
adult wasp is not carnivorous – it
feeds on the nectar
in flowers.

...VE BEETLE

...ne rove beetles
...cialize in feeding on
...ngtails. To catch
...h elusive prey the
...tle can flick out a
...g, sticky "tongue"
...pull an unwary
...ngtail into
...mouth.

*Beetle raises
tail before
attacking prey.*

Camouflage

Insects whose body coloring matches their background are almost impossible to see. This method of hiding is known as camouflage. One of the first rules of successful camouflage is to keep still, since movement can betray an insect to a sharp-eyed predator. Some insects use another type of camouflage called disruptive coloration. They disguise their body by breaking up its shape with stripes and blocks of color.

GRASSY DISGUISE
The stripe-winged grasshopper can be heard singing in meadow grasses, but its camouflaged body is very hard to spot.

Grasshopper kicks any attackers with its back legs.

DISRUPTIVE COLORATION
This tropical moth has disruptive coloration. The patterns on the wings break up their shape. A predator might notice the patterns, but not the whole moth.

BLENDING IN
This tropical bush cricket's color and shape help it to blend in with the foliage of the plants on which it lives in the rain forest.

This bush cricket lives in the Peruvian Amazon rain forest.

STILL HUNTER
Insect predators use camouflage so their prey cannot see them. The brown coloring of this mantid perfectly matches the brown leaf on which it sits. It completely surprises any prey which comes within striking distance.

Because of its brown coloring, the Indian leaf butterfly can rest only beside decaying, dried-out leaves.

Midvein on real leaf

Mantis is hard to spot.

Butterfly's head

Wing of butterfly

LEAF MIMIC
It is almost impossible to distinguish the Indian leaf butterfly from the other leaves where it rests. It looks just like a decaying leaf, complete with leaflike veins and mock fungus spots.

Bottom of wings are narrow to look like stalk of real leaf

Marking like midvein of real leaf

Warning coloration

Birds, mammals, and other intelligent predators learn through experience that some insects are poisonous or harmful. Such insects do not camouflage themselves. Instead they have brightly colored bodies which warn predators that they have an unpleasant taste or a nasty sting. The most common warning colors are red, yellow, and black. Any insect with those colors is probably poisonous.

BASKER MOTH
Moths that fly by day are often brightly colored, particularly when they taste unpleasant. The red, yellow, and black coloring of this basker moth tells birds that it is not a tasty meal.

PAINFUL REMINDER
The saddle-back caterpillar is eye-catching with its vivid coloring and grotesque appearance. No young bird would ever forget the caterpillar if it tried a mouthful of the poisonous, stinging spines.

Poisonous spines

Vivid green coloring across back

Bright spot

WARNING SPOTS
This assassin bug is easily seen because of the two bright spots on its back. These bold markings warn predators that there is a reason for them to stay away. The bug's weapon is a needle-sharp beak which can give a very painful bite.

EYESPOTS
This silk moth is camouflaged when its wings are closed. But when attacked by a predator, the moth flashes the eyespots on its hind wings. This startles the attacker briefly, and may give the moth time to escape.

Camouflaged front wings

Eyespot

POISONOUS BODY
This grasshopper tastes horrible. It gets its terrible flavor from eating poisonous plants and storing the poisons in its body. The yellow and black stripes advertise its unpleasantness to birds and other predators.

Grasshopper uses the spines on its legs for defense.

...es are black to ...lend with rest of coloring.

Mimicry

Predators usually avoid preying on dangerous animals. Many harmless insects take advantage of this by mimicking harmful creatures. Mimicking insects copy a dangerous animal's body shape and coloring. They also behave like the animal they're copying to make the disguise more convincing. Inedible objects, such as twigs and thorns, are also mimicked by insects.

The treehoppers move only when they need a fresh source of food.

Wasp has two wings, but the hover fly has four.

Wasp has a narrower waist than hover fly.

Hover fly resembles wasp in color, size, and shape.

WASP MIMIC
Hover flies cannot sting, so they find protection by mimicking the warning colors of wasps. They even hover like wasps. Although the disguise is not perfect, it is enough to persuade most animals to leave them alone.

HOVER FLY

WASP

THORN MIMICS
These treehoppers mimic green thorns, a disguise which seems to fool most predators. The treehoppers have piercing mouthparts and sit motionless for hours feeding on the sap of a plant.

Legs are held close to body.

Head

TWIG MIMIC
Inchworms, the larvae of geometrid moths, often mimic dead twigs. They feed at night and are almost unrecognizable as an insect by day, sticking out motionless at the end of a twig.

Legs of moth

Moth has same coloring as flower.

Hanging flower

Real twig

Prolegs at end of caterpillar clutch twig.

FLOWER MIMIC
Insects which are active by night need to rest by day. But resting insects are vulnerable, and the daylight makes it easier for predators to see them. To go unnoticed, this moth from Trinidad mimics the hanging flowers on a bush where it rests during the day.

WHERE INSECTS LIVE

INSECTS LIVE everywhere there is warmth and moisture. Many of the one million or more species have specialized habitat requirements. They can live only in particular places, and easily become extinct when humans change or destroy their surroundings. Other species are able to adapt to changing conditions; these adaptable insects often become pests.

TEMPERATE WOODLAND
The varied plant life and complex structure of temperate woodland provides insects with many different habitats. Trees, shrubs, and herbs all have flowers, fruits, and buds for insects to feed on, as well as stems and roots for insects to bore into.

GRASSLANDS AND HEATHLANDS
These habitats offer little shelter from bad weather. But they warm up quickly in the sun, and have a rich variety of flowering plants.

TOWNS AND GARDENS
Hundreds of insect species take advantage of human habitats. Insects find food and shelter in our roofs, cellars, food stores, kitchens, garbage cans, farms, and in our flower-filled gardens.

ARCTIC

EUROPE

ASIA

AFRICA

AUSTRALASIA

ANTARCTIC

DESERTS, SOIL, AND CAVES
Food and water are scarce in deserts. Dense soil makes it hard for insects to communicate and move. Caves are dark and may be very cold or hot and humid.

TROPICAL FORESTS
This is the richest habitat for insect species. Thousands of species of plants provide countless niches for insects to live in, from treetop fruits to dead leaves and twigs on the ground.

LAKES AND RIVERS
Freshwater insects are highly specialized. Their bodies have modified to allow them to swim and breathe underwater.

TEMPERATE WOODLAND

ABOUT THE HABITAT

FIELD SCABI
FLOWER

TEMPERATE WOODLANDS are often dominated by one tree species, such as oak, which is deciduous (the trees lose their leaves in winter). The types of insect found, and their numbers, will vary with the seasons, as well as with the types of tree species in the woodlands.

DRAINING
Forests in wetlands have many different plant species. But people often drain this habitat because it is good for farming. Draining kills plants such as milk-parsley, the only plant the English swallowtail butterfly will breed on. This beautiful insect is now rarely seen.

+1.4

Although the English swallowtail will lay eggs only on milk-parsley, adults eat a variety of flowers.

The woodland edge supports the greatest number of insect species.

Each pair of blue tits needs about 5,000 caterpillars to feed to their chicks.

In Britain, over 280 species of insect live on native oak trees.

Temperate rainforests in the northwestern United States are disappearing faster than tropical rainforests.

Bumblebees are very common in woodlands.

+2

FLOWERS
Woodlands contain many types of flower. These attract various species of insect, such as bumblebees, which nest in the ground in animal burrows and pollinate many woodland flowers.

Vaporer moth caterpillar is covered with tufts of hair.

VAPORER MOTH CATERPILLAR
This attractive caterpillar eats the leaves of many different trees in Europe and North America. It will also attack rosebushes and heather plants.

Processionary caterpillars are covered in poisonous hairs.

PROCESSIONS
Conifer forests have fewer types of plant and animal than deciduous forests, although some, such as processionary moth caterpillars, can be common. These are named for their habit of following each other head to tail.

OAK TREE

IN NORTH AMERICA and Europe, oak trees support a rich variety of insects. There are insects living on every part of the oak tree – the leaves, buds, flowers, fruits, wood, bark, and on decaying leaves and branches. All these insects provide food for the many birds and other animals found in oak woodland.

OAK TREE

GREEN OAK TORTRIX MOTH

CATERPILLAR

GREEN OAK TORTRIX

The green wings of the green oak tortrix moth camouflage the moth when it rests on a leaf. Green oak tortrix caterpillars are extremely common on oak trees. The caterpillars hide from hungry predators by rolling themselves up in a leaf.

+1.25

+2

Leaf roll around gre oak tortri caterpilla

Mine

MAKING A TUNNEL

The caterpillars of some sma moths tunnel between the upper and lower surfaces of leaf. They eat the green tiss between these surfaces as th tunnel, and leave a see-through trail called a mine.

+12

Chalcid wasp larvae have eaten the gall wasp larvae

GALLS

Oak trees have many tiny growths called galls. Galls are grown by the tree around eggs laid by gall wasps. When the eggs hatch, the gall provides food and shelter for up to 30 wasp larvae. Parasitic wasps called ‹alcid wasps sometimes burrow inside galls and lay ‹eir eggs beside the gall wasp eggs. When the ‹alcid larvae hatch they eat the gall wasp larvae.

CHALCID
WASP ON
GALL

‹UT WEEVILS

‹corns are used as food by
‹t weevils. They drill a
ble in an acorn with their
‹g, thin snout, and then
‹ their eggs inside. The
‹rvae feed inside the
‹orn, and this turns
‹e acorn
‹ack.

*Black
acorn*

ACORNS

Antenna

‹ng,
‹hin
‹nout

+4

NUT WEEVIL

TREE CANOPY

THE UPPER BRANCHES and leaves
of a tree are like a living green
umbrella, forming a canopy over
the lower plants. Countless
insects find their food in the
canopy and they are food for
many different birds.

*Inchworm
on leaf*

*Silken thread
suspends
inchworm.*

INCHWORMS
Some young birds like
to feed on inchworms,
the caterpillars of
Geometrid moths.
When in danger, inchworm
can drop from a leaf and ha
below by a silken thread.

*Very long antennae help
the cricket find its way
in the dark. They also alert
the cricket to the approach
of an enemy.*

*Compound
eye*

OAK BUSH CRICKETS
At night, male oak bush crickets drum
on leaves with their feet so that a
female oak bush cricket, like this one,
knows where to find a mate. The
cricket's green body blends in well
with its leafy surroundings.

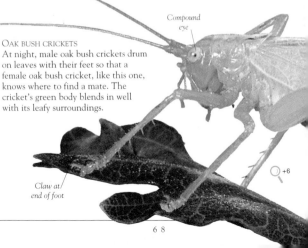

*Claw at
end of foot*

+6

EUROPEAN WASP

Wasps kill insects that destroy plants and fruit.

+2.7

Claw on end of foot for gripping surfaces

WASPS
A healthy woodland has a balance of prey and predators. Wasps grow up on a diet of chewed caterpillars collected in the tree canopy. In summer a wasp nest may contain several hundred wasps.

MALE PURPLE EMPEROR AT REST

Strong back legs can be used to kick enemies

Camouflaged underside of wings

−.5

PURPLE EMPEROR
This butterfly feeds on sap, honeydew, and liquids that ooze from dung and animal carcasses. A male purple emperor's territory is often at the top of the tallest tree in a wood. If a rival male enters another male's territory, the two fight in midair, clashing wings until one gives in.

MALE PURPLE EMPEROR

Wings are normally dark brown.

It is only when wings are at a certain angle to the light that they appear to be purple.

WOODLAND BUTTERFLIES

THE RICH VARIETY of habitats in woodland
supports many butterfly species.
Some live in the canopy; others
feed on low shrubs. But most
butterflies need sunshine and can be
found on flowers in sunny clearings.

SILVER-WASHED FRITILLARY
This butterfly lays its eggs
in cracks in the bark of
mossy tree trunks, close to
where violets are growing.
The caterpillars feed on
the leaves of these plants.

Brown upperside

Green undersid

GREEN HAIRSTREAK
Whether it is
sitting on a
branch or resting
on a leaf, the
green hairstreak butterfly is well
camouflaged. Its upperside is a woody
brown while its underside is a leafy green.

PURPLE
HAIRSTREAK
BUTTERFLY

Female

Male

Eyespots on underwings

PURPLE HAIRSTREA
High in the canop
of oak trees th
caterpillars of th
purple hairstrea
butterfly feed on flower
and young leave
Adult purple hairstreak
spend most of thei
lives in the treetops
feeding and sunbathin
with their wings ope

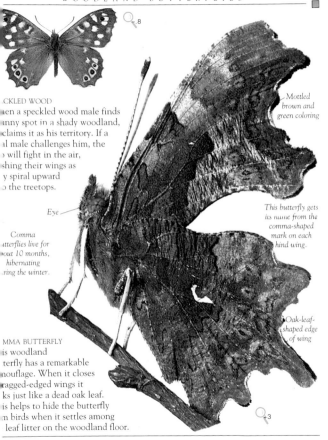

Mottled brown and green coloring

SPECKLED WOOD

When a speckled wood male finds a sunny spot in a shady woodland, he claims it as his territory. If a rival male challenges him, the two will fight in the air, flashing their wings as they spiral upward to the treetops.

Eye

This butterfly gets its name from the comma-shaped mark on each hind wing.

Comma butterflies live for about 10 months, hibernating during the winter.

Oak-leaf-shaped edge of wing

COMMA BUTTERFLY

This woodland butterfly has a remarkable camouflage. When it closes its ragged-edged wings it looks just like a dead oak leaf. This helps to hide the butterfly from birds when it settles among leaf litter on the woodland floor.

TREE TRUNKS AND BRANCHES

CRACKS IN THE bark of trees provide a hiding place fo
many species of insect. Some burrow into the wood
and live completely concealed from predators. Many
insects also live and feed among the different plant li
that grows on tree trunks and branches.

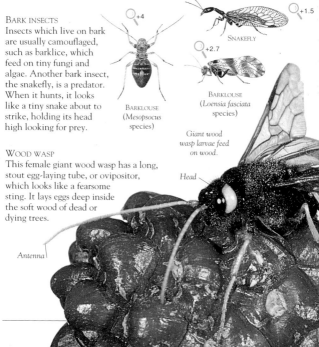

BARK INSECTS

Insects which live on bark
are usually camouflaged,
such as barklice, which
feed on tiny fungi and
algae. Another bark insect,
the snakefly, is a predator.
When it hunts, it looks
like a tiny snake about to
strike, holding its head
high looking for prey.

+4

BARKLOUSE
(*Mesopsocus*
species)

+1.5

SNAKEFLY

+2.7

BARKLOUSE
(*Loensia fasciata*
species)

*Giant wood
wasp larvae feed
on wood.*

WOOD WASP

This female giant wood wasp has a long,
stout egg-laying tube, or ovipositor,
which looks like a fearsome
sting. It lays eggs deep inside
the soft wood of dead or
dying trees.

Head

Antenna

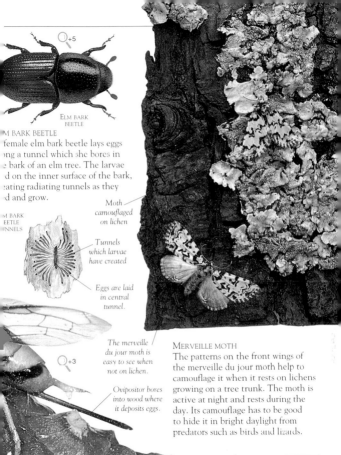

+5

ELM BARK
BEETLE

ELM BARK BEETLE
The female elm bark beetle lays eggs
along a tunnel which she bores in
the bark of an elm tree. The larvae
feed on the inner surface of the bark,
creating radiating tunnels as they
feed and grow.

ELM BARK
BEETLE
TUNNELS

Moth
camouflaged
on lichen

Tunnels
which larvae
have created

Eggs are laid
in central
tunnel.

The merveille
du jour moth is
easy to see when
not on lichen.

+3

Ovipositor bores
into wood where
it deposits eggs.

MERVEILLE MOTH
The patterns on the front wings of
the merveille du jour moth help to
camouflage it when it rests on lichens
growing on a tree trunk. The moth is
active at night and rests during the
day. Its camouflage has to be good
to hide it in bright daylight from
predators such as birds and lizards.

GROUND LEVEL

THE WOODLAND floor does not get much sunlight, so few plants grow there. Most insects at ground level feed on plant and animal debris falling from the canopy, or, if they are carnivorous, eat other insects.

ANT NEST
The wood ant is a voracious predator. Colonies build huge nests of plant debris, with a network of tunnels below ground providing a home for thousands of ants.

WOOD CRICKET
Most crickets are nocturnal (active at night). But the wood cricket is active on sunny days when it can be heard chirping loudly. It is unable to fly because of its short wings.

Strong jaws bite into prey.

WOOD ANT
Wood ants forage out from their nest for hundreds of yards, making distinct paths on the woodland floor. They catch huge numbers of insects and bring them to the nest in pieces as food for their young.

Ant can squirt poison from abdomen.

⊕+8

VIOLET GROUND BEETLE
This beetle can run fast on its long legs, catching other insects among the leaf litter. It hunts mainly at night and grips its prey with powerful jaws.

-1

STAG BEETLE
The larvae of stag beetles spend about three years feeding on rotting wood inside a dead tree. These handsome beetles are now becoming rare because dead wood is often cleared away and burned.

WHITE ADMIRALS
On sunny days, white admiral butterflies can be spotted near the ground feeding on the nectar of bramble flowers. They can often be seen in the morning sipping water from puddles. They spend much of their time in the tree canopy, basking in the sunshine.

+2.5

UPPERSIDE OF
WHITE ADMIRAL

UNDERSIDE OF
WHITE ADMIRAL

Antenna

Only male
stag beetles
have enlarged
jaws.

+3

GRASSLANDS AND HEATHLANDS

ABOUT THE HABITA

GRASSLANDS AND HEATHLANDS have no protective tree canopy, which means they change quickl with the weather – from hot and dry to windy, cold, or wet. These habitats are less complex than forest or woodland. They provide fewer dwelling places for insec since there is little wood to burrow into and hardly any le litter to dwell in.

This grass is called cocks-foot.

FIELD CHAFER

+1.2

FOOD SOURCE
Plant roots are an important food for insects in these habitats. Field chafer larvae eat roots, while the adults fly from plant to plant seeking a mate.

SPRINGTAILS
Cultivated grass fields, such as sport fields, support few insect species. Bu they do contain vast numbers of tiny insects called springtails. An area th size of a tennis court might be home up to three hundred million springta

CINNABAR MOTH

XFORD RAGWORT
weed called the
xford ragwort is a
mmon invader of
glected pasture in
rope. The cinnabar
oth lays its eggs on
is weed, and its
terpillars eat
e leaves.

GRASSLAND FACTS

- The grasslands of
  Argentina are called
  Pampas, or "plains" in
  the language of the
  native people.

- Long grasses grow on
  the prairies of the US.

- The Steppes (prairie-
  like lands) of Siberia
  have short
  grasses.

*The moth has
arning coloration
because it tastes
unpleasant.*

*An Oxford
ragwort is often
stripped of its leaves
by feeding caterpillars.*

CH IN PLANT LIFE
atural grassland and
athland have a huge
riety of grasses
d flowering
ants. These rich
abitats buzz with
sect life
the
mmer
onths.

CRANESBILL

RARE BUTTERFLY
The English large copper
butterfly was once common
in fenland but is now extinct.
This is a result of intensive
land development for
agriculture, which destroyed
the butterfly's food plant, the
great water dock.

GRASSLAND INSECTS

MOST INSECT species cannot survive in cultivated grass lands, such as garden lawns, since they usually contain only one type of grass. Also, weedkillers and other chemicals harm many insects. But natural grasslands, with their variety of plants, support thousands of insect species that have adapted to this open, windy habitat.

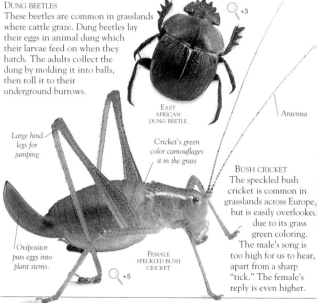

DUNG BEETLES
These beetles are common in grasslands where cattle graze. Dung beetles lay their eggs in animal dung which their larvae feed on when they hatch. The adults collect the dung by molding it into balls, then roll it to their underground burrows.

EAST AFRICAN DUNG BEETLE

+3

Antenna

Large hind legs for jumping

Cricket's green color camouflages it in the grass

BUSH CRICKET
The speckled bush cricket is common in grasslands across Europe, but is easily overlooked due to its grass green coloring. The male's song is too high for us to hear, apart from a sharp "tick." The female's reply is even higher.

Ovipositor puts eggs into plant stems.

FEMALE SPECKLED BUSH CRICKET

+5

ANTEATER

here are so many ants in
e grasslands of South
merica and Africa
at specialized
t-eating
ammals have
olved. They have
owerful claws to break open ant
sts, and long sticky tongues to
llect the ants.

ANTEATER

— .8

LARGE BLUE BUTTERFLY

This butterfly lays its eggs
on the wild thyme plant,
and the newly hatched
caterpillars feed on thyme
flowers. The caterpillars
attract red ants with a
special milk. The ants are
deceived into carrying the
caterpillars into their nest,
where the caterpillars eat
the ant eggs and larva.

*Ragwort
flowers*

+1.3

ARBLED WHITE BUTTERFLY

his butterfly can be found in a
riety of grassland habitats, including
assy areas inside woodland. Marbled
hites often gather in groups to
sk in the early morning and
rly evening sunshine.

*Mating
soldier beetles*

OLDIER BEETLES

ome insects feed on one particular
ower, while others, such as
oldier beetles, eat pollen from
arious flowers. These feeding
tes are also good places for
sects to find a mate.

— .3

HEATHLAND INSECTS

MANY BURROWING insects live in heathland since the soil is loose and easy to dig into. Heathland occurs in parts of the world with a climate of rainy winters and warm, dry summers. It has a rich mixture of plants, and the soil, which is often sandy, warms up quickly in the sunshine.

Butterfly is hard to spot in the grass.

GRAYLING BUTTERFLY
The tops of the wings of the grayling butterfly are bright colored, while their underside is mottled gray for camouflage on the ground. When resting it folds back its wings and sometimes leans toward the sun so it casts no shadow.

COMMON YELLOW DUNG FLY

🔍+4

Dung flies eat other insects, which they kill with piercing mouthparts.

DUNG FLY
Wherever cattle are grazing, insects will found breeding in the cattle's nutritious dung. Dung flies lay their eggs on freshly deposited cow pats. The maggots hatch a few hours later and start eating the dung

FIELD CRICKET

This sturdy cricket is a sun-loving insect, although it nests in a burrow underground. Males sit at the mouth of their burrow in summer chirping hour after hour to attract a mate, although this male has attracted a second male instead.

row

ER BEETLE

s brightly colored beetle has large eyes long legs. When it is warmed by the it can run and fly very quickly. It fierce predator that lives in a row in sandy soil, from which it dashes out to seize its insect prey.

Antenna

er beetles have
p, cutting jaws
r killing and
eating prey.

Eye

Long legs
for chasing
prey

The prey of the
er beetle includes
ther beetles and
grasshoppers.

Q +3.3

Antlion
larva
seizing ant

ANTLION LARVA

The larva of the antlion, a damselfly-like insect, often digs conical pits in sandy soils. Lying in wait at the bottom of its pit, the larva uses its long jaws to catch any small insect that falls in.

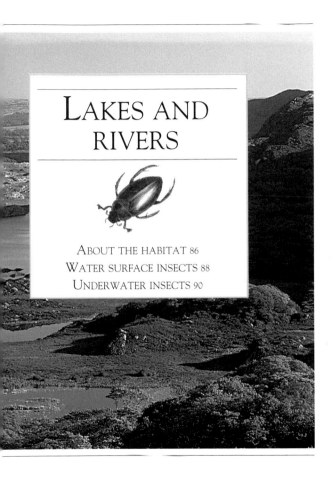

LAKES AND RIVERS

ABOUT THE HABITAT

INSECTS CAN be found in all sorts
of freshwater habitats: lakes,
fast-flowing streams, ponds,
puddles, damp moss, and wet
leaf litter. These insects have
many adaptations for surviving
in their watery homes.

*This case is made
of a mixture of
leaves and
stones.*

Q +3

*The stony case is
held together by silk
woven by the larva.*

Head

*Legs hold
onto plant.*

*Flowers attract
nectar-eating
insects.*

*The flat leaves have
a water-repellent waxy
covering so they don't
get waterlogged.*

CADDISFLY LARVAE
Insects can be swept away
fast-flowing water. Caddis
larvae build a c
around their body for protection. So
cases have long twigs sticking out sidew
to prevent fish from swallowing the

FRINGED WATERLILY
The tangled stems of the fringed
waterlily are a good hidin
place for pond insects.
Dragonflies also find the
leaves and stems a safe place o
which to lay their eggs.

8 6

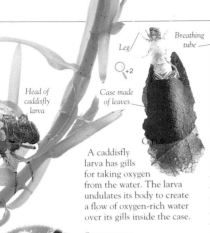

Breathing tube

Leg

Q_{+2}

Head of
caddisfly
larva

Case made
of leaves

A caddisfly
larva has gills
for taking oxygen
from the water. The larva
undulates its body to create
a flow of oxygen-rich water
over its gills inside the case.

WATER SCORPION
The water scorpion has a
breathing tube on its rear
end so it can breathe the
outside air while it is
underwater. Insects with
breathing tubes can
survive in warm ponds or
polluted waters that are
low in oxygen.

SPRINGTAILS
In corners of ponds
sheltered from the wind,
swarms of springtails
sometimes gather on the
surface of the water. They
feed on organic debris that has
blown into the pond.

FAST STREAMS
Insects that live in fast-
flowing streams have
streamlined bodies and
strong claws to help them
cling to stones. The water
that passes over their gills is
always rich in oxygen, but
cool temperatures mean that
larvae develop more slowly
than they would in a
shallow, sun-warmed pond.

LAKES AND RIVERS FACTS

• Fish populations
depend on plenty of
insects as food.

• Dragonfly larvae are
considered a delicacy in
New Guinea.

• Swarms of nonbiting
midges are sometimes
so dense over African
lakes that fishermen
have been suffocated.

WATER SURFACE INSECTS

A WATER SURFACE behaves like a skin due to a force called surface tension. This force enables certain insects to walk on the "skin," and others to hang just beneath it. Many of these insects are predators, and much of their food comes from the constant supply of flying insects which have fallen into the water.

+6

WHIRLIGIG

The whirligig beetle swims around and around very fast on the water surface. It hunts insects trapped on the surface tension. The whirligig's eyes are divided into two halves, allowing it to see both above and below the water surface at the same time.

BACKSWIMMER

Using its oar-shaped back legs, this water bug swims along upside down as it patrols in search of insects trapped on the water's surface. The backswimmer is a hungry hunter and will even attack fish and young frogs.

Piercing mouthparts inject poison into prey and suck out the prey's body fluids.

Large, compound eyes for spotting prey

+5

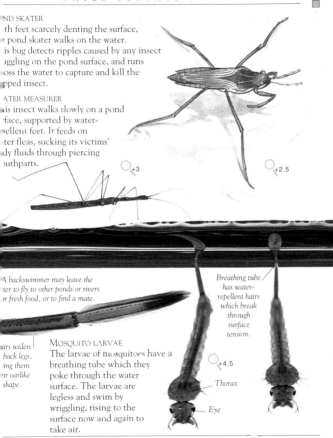

[PO]ND SKATER

[Wi]th feet scarcely denting the surface,
[a] pond skater walks on the water.
[Th]is bug detects ripples caused by any insect
[stru]ggling on the pond surface, and runs
[acr]oss the water to capture and kill the
[tra]pped insect.

[W]ATER MEASURER

[Th]is insect walks slowly on a pond
[sur]face, supported by water-
[rep]ellent feet. It feeds on
[wa]ter fleas, sucking its victims'
[bo]dy fluids through piercing
[mo]uthparts.

+3

+2.5

A backswimmer may leave the
[wa]ter to fly to other ponds or rivers
[fo]r fresh food, or to find a mate.

*Breathing tube
has water-
repellent hairs
which break
through
surface
tension.*

[Ha]irs widen
[the] back legs,
[giv]ing them
[the]ir oarlike
[sh]ape.

MOSQUITO LARVAE

The larvae of mosquitoes have a
breathing tube which they
poke through the water
surface. The larvae are
legless and swim by
wriggling, rising to the
surface now and again to
take air.

+4.5

Thorax

Eye

UNDERWATER INSECTS

MANY OF THE insects that live underwater are carnivorous, either hunting their prey or scavenging. Some of these insects are fierce, sometimes killing prey larger than themselves.

DIVING BEETLE
The great diving beetle collects air from the water surface and stores it under its wings 🔍 +1.5 to breathe as it swims underwater.

This mighty beetle can catch insects, small fish and tadpoles.

Nymph waits for prey to swim past.
🔍 +1.5

The great diving beetle sometimes flies from one pond to another.

Antenna

Water plants provide food and shelter for water insects.

DAMSELFLY NYMPH

LARVAL CASES
Caddisfly larvae sometimes use pieces of plant to make their protective cases. This body armor also acts as camouflage.

Pieces of plant

MAYFLY NYMPH
A mayfly spends one year as a nymph living underwater before it leaves the water to become an adult. The nymph breathes through gills along the side of its abdomen.

🔍 +0

ADULT DRAGONFLY

Male darter dragonflies perch
on plants that emerge from the
water. They fiercely attack and
drive away any rival males of
the same species, but attempt
to mate with any female darter
dragonfly that flies past.

$_-.7$

DRAGONFLY EGGS

Darter dragonflies scatter their
eggs in the water. The eggs are
surrounded by a sticky, jelly-
like substance, and hatch
after a few days.

*Jelly holds
eggs in place.*

$_-.7$

BEETLE LARVA

The larva of the great diving beetle
injects juices into prey with its jaws.
The juices turn the prey's insides
into liquid for the larva to suck out.

DRAGONFLY NYMPH

Dragonfly nymphs breathe by
pumping water in and out of their
rear end, where they have
complex gills.

$_{+1.5}$

TROPICAL
FOREST

ORCHID

ABOUT THE HABITAT

INSECTS THRIVE in the humid heat and flourishing plant life of tropical forests. These forests have a complex structure that provides many habitats for insects. Trees vary in shape and size; vines and dead branches are everywhere, and thick leaf litter covers the ground.

ORCHIDS
Tropical forests contain a spectacular variety of plants – there are about 25,000 species of orchid alone. It is quite dark beneath the forest canopy and orchids are strongly scented to help insects find them.

EPIPHYTES
Many plants grow on the trunks and branches of trees where birds have wiped seeds from their beaks. These tree-dwelling plants, called epiphytes, provide extra habitats for insects.

INSECT PREDATORS
A tropical forest is a rich habitat for birds as well as insects. Tropical birds feed on countless insects each day. This high rate of predation is a major reason for the evolution of camouflage and mimicry in tropical insects.

FRUITY NOURISHMENT
Some tropical butterflies live for several months. An important source of fuel for their continued activity is rotting fruit and dung on the forest floor. This gives them not only sugars for energy, but also amino acids and vitamins needed for survival.

Until recently, this insect was known only from dull brown museum specimens.

Blue face

Red eye

TROPICAL FORESTS

Bright colors are typical of tropical forests, and they can be seen in both the plant and animal life. This Central American grasshopper looks as if it would be easy to spot with its multicolored body, but it is camouflaged among the shining leaves of the forest trees.

The bright colors of this grasshopper surprised even entomologists.

Bright green abdomen

+2

The cricket loses its blue color when it dies.

TROPICAL FOREST FACTS

• Tropical forests cover about five percent of the Earth's land surface.

• They contain over half of all living species.

• Around 1,200 species of butterfly have been recorded in one forest in southern Peru.

• Over half the world's rainforest has been cut since 1945.

IN THE CANOPY

THERE IS WARMTH, light, and plenty of food to eat in the canopy of tropical trees. The canopy provides living space for thousands of insect species. In one day 3,000 different species were collected from a single tree in a forest in Borneo.

BRIGHT BEETLES
Many beetle species living on the leaves of tropical trees are brightly colored. These gaily colored beetles are difficult to see when they are sitting on shiny tree leaves in bright sunshine.

THREE L
BEETLE

CICADAS
A male cicada produces a very loud mating song with drumlike organs called tymbals on both sides of its abdomen. A cavity beside each tymbal amplifies the sound. In the mating season, cicada males sing in the canopy, filling tropical forests with their shrill song.

Spines are spiked and poisonous.

OG BEETLE

his vividly colored
weled frog beetle is
obably less noticeable
the bright sunshine
its leafy habitat.
espite its name,
e froglike hind
gs are not used for
mping, but for
olding onto a female
ile mating.

*Froglike
hind leg*

+0

-2.5

VIOLIN BEETLE

Little is know about the curious
violin beetle, which got its name
because of its violin-like shape.
It is very flat, and has been found
living between layers of shelf
fungi on tree trunks in
Indonesian forests.

*Six simple eyes on either
side of the head can sense
whether it is light or dark.*

+4

POISON SPINES

The body of the
postman butterfly
caterpillar contains
poisons. It gets the
poisons from chemicals
in the leaves of the
passionflower vines
that it eats. The
prickly spines remind
birds to avoid it.

PASSIONFLOWER

NESTS IN THE CANOPY

WITH SO MANY insects feeding in the forest canopy, it is not surprising that the insect-eating ants and wasps build their nests there. But these ants and wasps are in turn hunted by mammals and lizards, so their nests must give protection.

Nest is m of paper materia

GREEN WEAVER ANTS

Each green weaver ant colony has several nests made of leaves. To make a nest, the ants join forces to pull leaves together and sew the edges. They sew using silk which the larvae produce when they are squeezed by the adult ants. These carnivorous ants hunt through the tree canopy, catching other insects and carrying the prey in pieces back to the ants' nests.

Ants pulling leaves together.

WASP NESTS

Each wasp species makes a different type of nest. This ne from South America has been cut in half to reveal the "floo which house the larvae. Ther one small opening at the bott where the wasps defend the n from invading ants.

This nest hangs from a branch of a tree.

There may be half a million ants in one weaver ant colony.

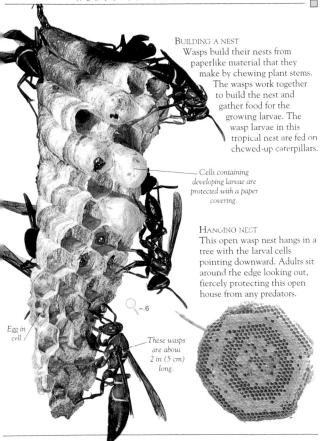

BUILDING A NEST

Wasps build their nests from paperlike material that they make by chewing plant stems. The wasps work together to build the nest and gather food for the growing larvae. The wasp larvae in this tropical nest are fed on chewed-up caterpillars.

Cells containing developing larvae are protected with a paper covering.

HANGING NEST

This open wasp nest hangs in a tree with the larval cells pointing downward. Adults sit around the edge looking out, fiercely protecting this open house from any predators.

—.6

Egg in cell

These wasps are about 2 in (5 cm) long.

BRILLIANT BUTTERFLIES

MANY TROPICAL butterflies are large and brilliantly colored, which ought to make it easy for predators to catch them. But they fly rapidly and erratically, flash their bright colors in the sun, and then seem to disappear, darting into the deep shade of the forest.

BLUE MORPHO
The iridescent blue of South American morpho butterflies is so vivid it can be seen from a great distance. But its underwings are a muddy brown for camouflage when feeding on the ground.

SOUTHEAST ASIAN MOTH
The vivid colors of this southeast Asian moth shows that some day-flying moths can be as colorful as butterflies. The bright colors warn predators that this moth is poisonous.

NERO BUTTERFLY
The bright yellow Nero butterfly drinks from streams and puddles near mammal dung. This habit is common in butterflies of tropical forests, and supplies them with nutrients that are not available in flowers.

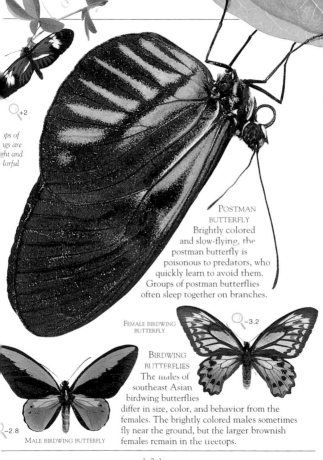

ps of
gs are
ht and
lorful

Q_{+2}

POSTMAN
BUTTERFLY
Brightly colored
and slow-flying, the
postman butterfly is
poisonous to predators, who
quickly learn to avoid them.
Groups of postman butterflies
often sleep together on branches.

FEMALE BIRDWING
BUTTERFLY

$Q_{-3.2}$

BIRDWING
BUTTERFLIES
The males of
southeast Asian
birdwing butterflies
differ in size, color, and behavior from the
females. The brightly colored males sometimes
fly near the ground, but the larger brownish
females remain in the treetops.

$_{-2.8}$
MALE BIRDWING BUTTERFLY

TROPICAL BUTTERFLIES

THOUSANDS OF butterfly species live in
tropical forests. Each butterfly has to
recognize members of its own specie
among all the others in order to mate
They find each other by sight –
butterflies have a good sense of color-
and by smell.

Q-.6

Tail brush

USING SCENTS

Striped blue crow butterfly
males have a yellow brush
at the end of their
abdomen. When a male
has found a female, he uses
his brush to dust scented
scales on her. The arousing
scent encourages the
female to mate with him.

SCENT DETECTORS

Butterflies and moths detect
smells with their antennae.
Each antenna has thousands
of microscopic sensory
organs. These respond to
airborne scent molecules,
triggering nerve cells in the
antennae to send signals to
the insect's brain.

MOTH ANTENNA

Scent chemicals
stimulate nerves in
the antennae.

Q-2.5

SITTING TOGETHER

At sunny spots in the forest,
butterflies gather at muddy puddles to
drink water and salts. Butterflies of the
same species usually sit together, so that
white-colored species form one group,
blue another, and so on.

Postman butterflies and small postman butterflies are two different species. But they share the same wing patterns in different parts of South America.

SMALL POSTMAN BUTTERFLY
FROM SOUTHERN ECUADOR

POSTMAN BUTTERFLY
FROM SOUTHERN ECUADOR

SMALL POSTMAN BUTTERFLY
FROM SOUTHERN BRAZIL

POSTMAN BUTTERFLY
FROM SOUTHERN BRAZIL

SMALL POSTMAN BUTTERFLY
FROM WESTERN BRAZIL

POSTMAN BUTTERFLY
FROM WESTERN BRAZIL

COPYING PATTERNS

Sometimes two or more different species of poisonous butterfly – such as the postman and the small postman – share the same wing pattern. This type of mimicry protects both species, because birds only need to learn that one species is poisonous to avoid the other.

HORNED BEETLES

WITH SO MANY millions of insects in tropical forests, individuals must sometimes compete for the best living space in which to mate and lay eggs. Horned beetles have horns which they use as weapons in battle. A male may lock horns with other males to claim a good territory, and then attract females to him.

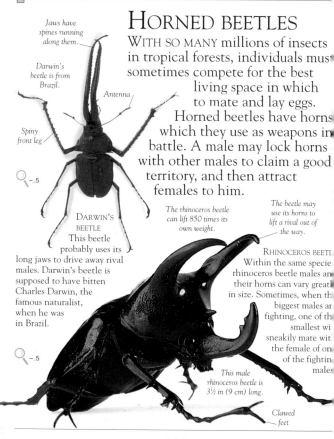

Jaws have spines running along them.

Darwin's beetle is from Brazil.

Antenna

Spiny front leg

○ -.5

DARWIN'S BEETLE
This beetle probably uses its long jaws to drive away rival males. Darwin's beetle is supposed to have bitten Charles Darwin, the famous naturalist, when he was in Brazil.

○ -.5

The rhinoceros beetle can lift 850 times its own weight.

The beetle may use its horns to lift a rival out of the way.

RHINOCEROS BEETLE
Within the same species rhinoceros beetle males and their horns can vary greatly in size. Sometimes, when the biggest males are fighting, one of the smallest will sneakily mate with the female of one of the fighting males.

This male rhinoceros beetle is 3½ in (9 cm) long.

Clawed feet

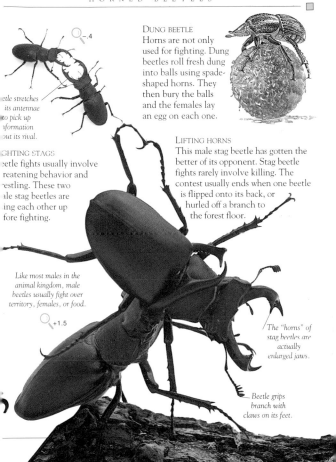

etle stretches
its antennae
o pick up
formation
out its rival.

DUNG BEETLE

Horns are not only
used for fighting. Dung
beetles roll fresh dung
into balls using spade-
shaped horns. They
then bury the balls
and the females lay
an egg on each one.

GHTING STAGS

eetle fights usually involve
reatening behavior and
estling. These two
ale stag beetles are
ing each other up
fore fighting.

LIFTING HORNS

This male stag beetle has gotten the
better of its opponent. Stag beetle
fights rarely involve killing. The
contest usually ends when one beetle
is flipped onto its back, or
hurled off a branch to
the forest floor.

*Like most males in the
animal kingdom, male
beetles usually fight over
territory, females, or food.*

*The "horns" of
stag beetles are
actually
enlarged jaws.*

Beetle grips
branch with
claws on its feet.

THE LARGEST INSECTS

SOME OF THE largest insects live in tropical forests, where the warm temperatures and abundance of food allow them to grow quickly. But insects cannot grow very large, since their simple breathing system could not cope with a large body. Also, big insects would be easy prey for birds and mammals.

ATLAS MOTH
With a wingspan of 6 in (15 cm), the atlas moth has the largest wing area of all insects. Silvery patch on each wing shine like mirrors.

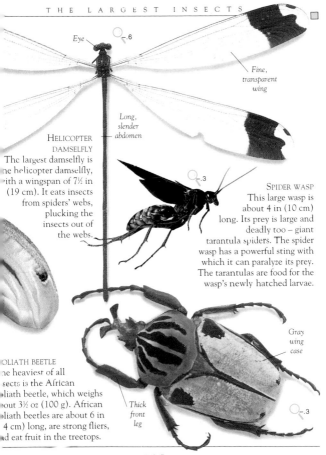

Eye

○—.6

Fine,
transparent
wing

Long,
slender
abdomen

HELICOPTER
DAMSELFLY
The largest damselfly is
the helicopter damselfly,
with a wingspan of 7½ in
(19 cm). It eats insects
from spiders' webs,
plucking the
insects out of
the webs.

○—.3

SPIDER WASP
This large wasp is
about 4 in (10 cm)
long. Its prey is large and
deadly too – giant
tarantula spiders. The spider
wasp has a powerful sting with
which it can paralyze its prey.
The tarantulas are food for the
wasp's newly hatched larvae.

Gray
wing
case

GOLIATH BEETLE
The heaviest of all
insects is the African
goliath beetle, which weighs
about 3½ oz (100 g). African
goliath beetles are about 6 in
(14 cm) long, are strong fliers,
and eat fruit in the treetops.

Thick
front
leg

○—.3

STICK AND LEAF INSECTS

A TROPICAL FOREST is alive with animals, most of which eat insects. To survive, insects adopt many strategies. Stick and leaf insects hide from predators by keeping still and resembling their background of leaves and sticks.

STICK INSECTS
Some stick insects are slender, brown, or green, just like the twigs and leaf stalks they sit on. Other species are shorter and fatter, with spines and other projections. These often look like curled dead leaves.

Winged male of Macleay's spectre

Wingless female of Macleay's spectre

Indian stick insect

Spiny green nymph

LEAF MIMICS
Javanese leaf insects are leaf mimics. They have body markings which look like the midrib and veins of a leaf. Brown marks like those on a dying leaf add to the disguise.

5

Imitation hole in "dying leaf"

Leg

n resting on branch, a anese stick ect curls its to look like e leaves it s beside.

Head

Imitation midrib

Body is almost as slim as a real leaf.

Real leaf

3

Undeveloped wings indicate that this insect is immature.

Green and brown coloring like a fading leaf

SPINY STICK INSECT
Good disguise is not just about appearance: it involves using the right behavior in the right place. This spiny stick insect is easily seen on the white background of this page. But if it were sitting in a bush and swaying gently like dead leaf, even a sharp-eyed bird may miss it.

ARMIES ON THE GROUND

ANTS ARE THE dominant creatures of tropical forests
They live in colonies made up of any number from
20 individuals to many thousands. Ants are mostly
carnivorous. Some species make slaves of other ant
species by invading their
nest and killing their queen

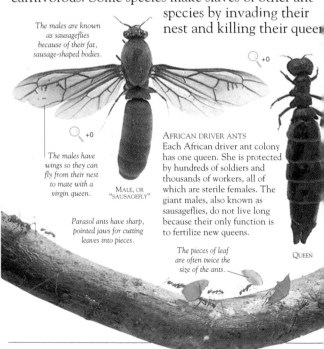

*The males are known
as sausageflies
because of their fat,
sausage-shaped bodies.*

+0

*The males have
wings so they can
fly from their nest
to mate with a
virgin queen.*

MALE, OR
"SAUSAGEFLY"

+0

AFRICAN DRIVER ANTS
Each African driver ant colony
has one queen. She is protected
by hundreds of soldiers and
thousands of workers, all of
which are sterile females. The
giant males, also known as
sausageflies, do not live long
because their only function is
to fertilize new queens.

QUEEN

*Parasol ants have sharp,
pointed jaws for cutting
leaves into pieces.*

*The pieces of leaf
are often twice the
size of the ants.*

DRIVER ANTS MARCHING

These ants get their name from the way a colony sweeps through an area catching all the insects it can find. They move their nests from place to place regularly, unlike most ants which have a permanent nest and territory.

+3

Beetle pupae are among the prey of driver ants

CARRYING PREY

Ants in a column collaborate to cut large insects they have caught into smaller pieces. This is so they can carry their food back to the nest. Smaller prey can be carried whole.

ATTENTIVE SOLDIER

Driver ant soldiers have very large jaws. Often they can be seen standing beside a marching column of ants with their jaws wide open, waiting to attack intruders such as parasitic flies.

Ant returning for more leaves

PARASOL ANTS

These South American ants are not carnivorous. They feed on fungus which they cultivate in huge underground nests. The fungus is grown on pieces of leaf which the ants bring to the nest.

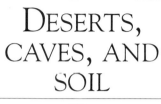

DESERTS, CAVES, AND SOIL

ABOUT THE HABITAT

SOME INSECTS flourish in habitats where it is difficul
for living things to survive. Desert habitats, for
example, lack water and have very high temperature
Caves are dark and lack plant life for food. Life in so
makes communication, by both
scent and sight, difficult
for insects.

A spike on the larva's back anchors it to the wall of the burrow.

HIDING IN SOIL

Life in the soil is only a passir
phase for some insect species.
This tiger beetle larva hides
underground by day. At night
waits in its vertical tunnel wit
its jaws projecting at the grou
surface, and snatches passing
insects to devour in its burro

CAVE DWELLER

This cockroach lives all its
life in the dark. Like other
cave creatures, it feeds on
debris from the outside
world. Bat dung, dead
animals, and pieces of
plants washed into the
cave provide the
cockroach with its
nourishment.

DESERT BEETLE
The lack of water in deserts forces insects to find ingenious ways of obtaining moisture. This darkling beetle lives in the Namib Desert, where sea winds bring mists each night. The beetle holds its abdomen high to catch the moisture, which then runs down into its mouth.

DESERT HEAT
The hot and dry days in deserts can lead to rapid water loss and death for animals. Most living creatures hide under stones or in the sand to avoid drying out. These animals are active at night when it is much cooler.

DESERT FACTS

• The Sahara Desert is spreading at a rate of 3 miles (5 km) per year.

• In deserts the temperature may range from 90°F (30°C) in the day to below 32°F (0°C) at night.

• Caves are a nearly constant temperature throughout the year.

• 20% of the Earth's land surface is desert.

CACTUS FLOWER

DESERT PLANTS
Rain may not fall in a desert for months, or even years. Most desert plants store water so they can survive, and some desert animals rely on these plants for food. But many animals, including some insects, migrate in search of rain and the plant growth it produces.

DESERT INSECTS

HOT, DRY DESERTS are dangerous places in which to live. Animals often die from sunstroke and dehydrati (drying out). To prevent this, insects avoid the sun b staying in the shade or burrowing in the sand. Some insects have special methods of collecting water. Mar feed only at night, because the surface of the sand is too hot for them to walk on during the day.

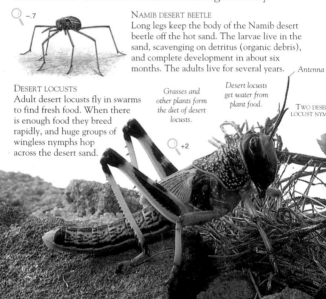

×.7

NAMIB DESERT BEETLE
Long legs keep the body of the Namib desert beetle off the hot sand. The larvae live in the sand, scavenging on detritus (organic debris), and complete development in about six months. The adults live for several years.

Antenna

DESERT LOCUSTS
Adult desert locusts fly in swarms to find fresh food. When there is enough food they breed rapidly, and huge groups of wingless nymphs hop across the desert sand.

Grasses and other plants form the diet of desert locusts.

Desert locusts get water from plant food.

TWO DESE LOCUST NYM

×+2

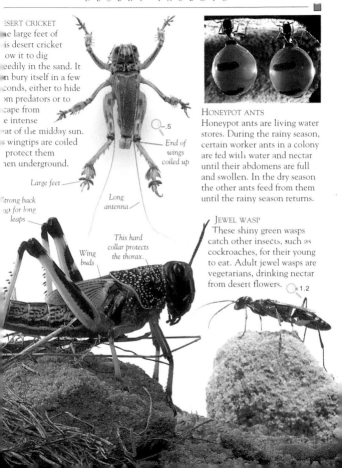

DESERT CRICKET
The large feet of
this desert cricket
allow it to dig
speedily in the sand. It
can bury itself in a few
seconds, either to hide
from predators or to
escape from
the intense
heat of the midday sun.
Its wingtips are coiled
to protect them
when underground.

.5

End of
wings
coiled up

Large feet

Strong back
legs for long
leaps

Long
antenna

Wing
buds

This hard
collar protects
the thorax.

HONEYPOT ANTS
Honeypot ants are living water
stores. During the rainy season,
certain worker ants in a colony
are fed with water and nectar
until their abdomens are full
and swollen. In the dry season
the other ants feed from them
until the rainy season returns.

JEWEL WASP
These shiny green wasps
catch other insects, such as
cockroaches, for their young
to eat. Adult jewel wasps are
vegetarians, drinking nectar
from desert flowers. ×1.2

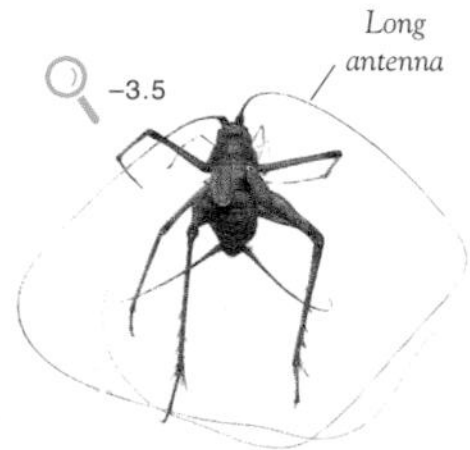

CAVE INSECTS

No plants can grow in the dark, inhospitable depths of caves, where the Sun's rays cannot reach. Despite this, cave-dwelling insects still manage to find enough food. Bat droppings, material washed in by floods, and the fungi that often grow on this decaying material all provide nourishment.

Long antenna

−3.5

AFRICAN CRICKET
Some insects have developed very long antennae to make up for lack of vision in dark caves. This African cricket has the longest antennae for its body size of any insect.

Long back legs for jumping out of danger

FEMALE AFRICAN CAVE CRICKET

Two sensitive spines, called cerci, can detect enemies approaching from behind.

Cricket uses its ovipositor (egg-laying tube) to lay eggs in soil.

+2.5

r some insects,
ves provide shelter
m the uncomfortable
ather conditions. During
ld northern winters a
ve is an ideal place
· peacock butterflies
hibernate.

*Dark underside of
wings camouflages the
eacock butterfly as it
hibernates.*

*Top of wings
are brightly
colored.*

–.8

PEACOCK BUTTERFLY

COCKROACH

Cave-dwelling cockroaches eat bat droppings
and bat carcasses, as well as mites and fungi.
Cockroaches often eat each other, too. Caves
make an ideal home for cockroaches since
they love dark, damp places.

+3

VE CRICKET
·ickets living in caves
ve smaller eyes and paler
·dies than crickets living
sunlight. Cave crickets
·ed all year because the
mperature and the amount
food in the cave
y constant.

*Very long,
sensitive
antennae*

SURINAM
COCKROACH

SOIL INSECTS

WHEN PLANTS and animals die, their remains usually get absorbed into the soil. Insects that live in soil are among the most important creatures on Earth because they help to recycle these remains, releasing their nutrients and so helping new crops and forests to grow. Soil insects are also an important food for many mammals and birds.

BEETLE LARVA
Roots and decaying tree trunks provide food for many types of insect larva, such as this beetle grub. The grub breathes through holes called spiracles, which are along the side of its body. Although there is not very much air underground, there is enough for insects.

Spiracle

Pupa

GOOD HABITAT
Living in soil has advantages. Insec are unlikely to dehydrate, and ther is plenty of food in plant roots and decaying plants. This spurge hawk-moth pupa has sharp plates on its abdomen which help it climb to th surface just before the adult emerge

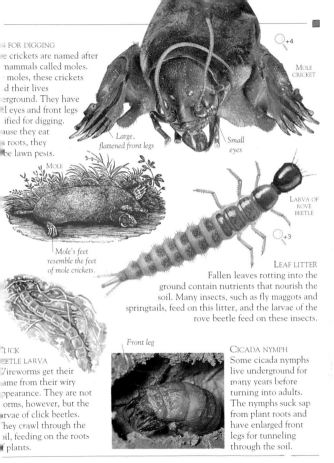

S FOR DIGGING

e crickets are named after
mammals called moles.
moles, these crickets
d their lives
erground. They have
l eyes and front legs
ified for digging.
use they eat
roots, they
be lawn pests.

MOLE
CRICKET

+4

*Large,
flattened front legs*

*Small
eyes*

MOLE

*Mole's feet
resemble the feet
of mole crickets.*

LARVA OF
ROVE
BEETLE

+3

LEAF LITTER

Fallen leaves rotting into the
ground contain nutrients that nourish the
soil. Many insects, such as fly maggots and
springtails, feed on this litter, and the larvae of the
rove beetle feed on these insects.

LICK
ETLE LARVA
Vireworms get their
ame from their wiry
pearance. They are not
orms, however, but the
rvae of click beetles.
hey crawl through the
il, feeding on the roots
plants.

Front leg

CICADA NYMPH
Some cicada nymphs
live underground for
many years before
turning into adults.
The nymphs suck sap
from plant roots and
have enlarged front
legs for tunneling
through the soil.

TOWNS AND
GARDENS

ABOUT THE HABITAT

SINCE INSECTS HAVE managed to make homes for themselves in practically every natural habitat, it is not surprising that they have turned human habitats into their homes, too. Insects live in our houses, feeding in our furniture, clothes, foodstores, and garbage dumps. Our gardens and farms are also teeming with insect life, nourished by the abundance of flowers, fruits and vegetables.

Colorado beetle

–1.4

POTATO PESTS
When potatoes were brought to Europe from South America, the Colorado beetle came with them. This insect eats potato plant leaves, and can cause great damage to crops.

Leaves of potato plant

Potato

CABBAGE EATERS
Cabbage white butterflies lay eggs on cabbage plants so the larvae can eat the leaves. Farms provide acres of cabbages, and the butterflies become pests since they breed at an unnaturally high rate because of the abundance of food.

WASPS IN OUR HOMES

The roofs of our houses keep us warm and dry, but they also provide ideal conditions for wasps' nests. Wasps are useful to us in summer since they catch our garden insect pests to feed to their young.

Nest hangs from rafters.

[IN]SECT INFESTATIONS

[Pe]sts such as cockroaches are [qu]ick to make use of any food [wh]ich we waste. Uncovered or [spi]lled food in kitchens allows [th]ese insects to thrive, and can [ca]use an infestation that [is h]ard to eliminate.

R+0

GREENHOUSES

In temperate countries, tropical insects often thrive in greenhouses, which reproduce tropical conditions. Butterfly farms use this principle to breed exotic insects for us to look at and enjoy.

TOWNS AND GARDENS FACTS

• More than 1,800 insect species were found in a typical English garden.

• Fewer than one percent of cockroach species are considered to be pests.

• Peacock butterflies often spend the winter in garden sheds.

The monarch butterfly is bred on butterfly farms.

HOUSEHOLD INSECTS

SINCE PREHISTORIC times, insects have lived in huma
homes, attracted by warmth, shelter, and food. Thes
insects eat our food, our furniture, and some even ea
our carpets. Parasitic insects also live in our homes,
feeding on the human inhabitants.

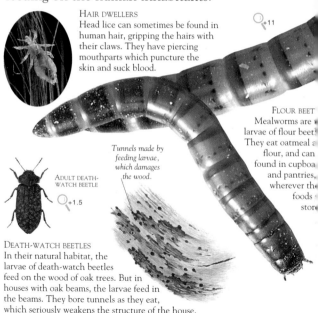

HAIR DWELLERS
Head lice can sometimes be found in
human hair, gripping the hairs with
their claws. They have piercing
mouthparts which puncture the
skin and suck blood.

+11

FLOUR BEET
Mealworms are
larvae of flour beet
They eat oatmeal a
flour, and can
found in cupboa
and pantries,
wherever th
foods
stor

*Tunnels made by
feeding larvae,
which damages
the wood.*

ADULT DEATH-
WATCH BEETLE

+1.5

DEATH-WATCH BEETLES
In their natural habitat, the
larvae of death-watch beetles
feed on the wood of oak trees. But in
houses with oak beams, the larvae feed in
the beams. They bore tunnels as they eat,
which seriously weakens the structure of the house.

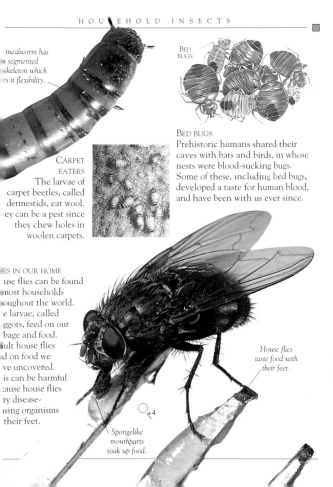

*mealworm has
segmented
skeleton which
s it flexibility.*

BED
BUGS

CARPET
EATERS
The larvae of
carpet beetles, called
dermestids, eat wool.
ey can be a pest since
they chew holes in
woolen carpets.

BED BUGS
Prehistoric humans shared their
caves with bats and birds, in whose
nests were blood-sucking bugs.
Some of these, including bed bugs,
developed a taste for human blood,
and have been with us ever since.

ES IN OUR HOME
use flies can be found
most households
oughout the world.
e larvae, called
ggots, feed on our
bage and food.
ult house flies
d on food we
ve uncovered.
is can be harmful
:ause house flies
ry disease-
ising organisms
their feet.

*House flies
taste food with
their feet.*

+4

*Spongelike
mouthparts
soak up food.*

GARDEN INSECTS

A GARDEN IS a good place to watch and study insects. Many different insects are attracted into gardens to feed on the flowers, vegetables, and other plants. Some predatory insects come to eat the plant-eating insects. But most garden insects are just tourists, feeding on flower nectar they pass through.

ROVE BEETLES
Rove beetles hunt at night, scouring the garden for insects to eat. These large beetles are common in compost piles, scurrying away from the daylight when the compost is turned.

+2.5

GARDENER'S FRIENDS
Hover flies hover in front of flowers on hot, sunny days as they feed on nectar. They are particularly attracted to thistle flowers. Hover fly larvae are the gardener's friends, feeding voraciously on plant-damaging aphids.

+3

Eye

Antenna

...WK MOTH

...caterpillars of
...k moths can be
...ognized by their
...rt, erect "tail." Most
...lt hawk moths fly at
...t, hovering in front of
...ers to gather nectar with
...ir long tongues.

SILVER-STRIPED HAWK
MOTH CATERPILLAR

"Tail"

+0

Eyespot

*Caterpillar has
eyespots to frighten
off predators.*

*Fuchsia
flower*

...ARDEN GRASSHOPPER

...e common field grasshopper is widespread in
...rope on short grass in sunny places, and often
...ds a home in gardens. Like tropical locusts,
...mmon field grasshoppers sometimes migrate in
...arms, but on a much smaller scale.

RED
ADMIRAL

...OD FOR BUTTERFLIES

...e flower border of a garden is like a filling
...tion for passing butterflies. They feed on
...ctar to give them energy as they search for
...itable mates or plants on which to lay eggs.

*Butterflies
often stop to
sunbathe for
a while.*

−.3

PEACOCK

−.6

SILVER-SPOTTED
SKIPPER

−.3

FRIENDS AND FOES

THE RELATIONSHIP between insects and
humans is not always good. Many inse
are useful to us, although others are
pests. We destroy their habitats, and
deny other wild animals of food.
   Ecology, involving the study of the
balance between our needs and the
needs of other animals and plants,
helps us to understand this conflic

*Aphids drink
the rose's sap. This
may kill the rose,
because the sap
is like the
plant's blood.*

APHIDS
Aphids are major pests o
our food plants and flowe
Some aphid species are
common on roses, while
others spread diseases
which ruin potatoes and
strawberries, as well as
many other food crops.

*Intricate
pattern of
veins in wings*

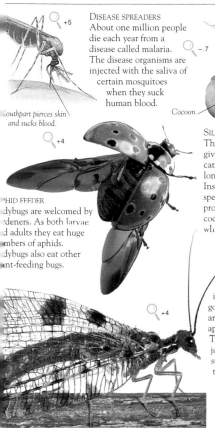

DISEASE SPREADERS
About one million people die each year from a disease called malaria. The disease organisms are injected with the saliva of certain mosquitoes when they suck human blood.

Mouthpart pierces skin and sucks blood.

Moth

Cocoon

SILK PROVIDERS
The silk we use in clothes is given to us by silk moth caterpillars. Silk moths no longer occur in the wild. Instead, they are bred in special farms. The caterpillars produce the silk to form cocoons that protect them when they pupate.

APHID FEEDER
Ladybugs are welcomed by gardeners. As both larvae and adults they eat huge numbers of aphids. Ladybugs also eat other plant-feeding bugs.

PEST EATERS
Lacewings are delicate insects, often with shining golden eyes. Their larvae are voracious predators of aphids and other plant lice. They have long, tubular jaws through which they suck the body contents of their prey. Lacewing larvae hide themselves from predators by sticking the remains of their prey onto small hairs on their back.

BEES AND POLLINATION

BEES AND PLANTS depend on each other.
Plants need bees to carry pollen
between flowers to produce seeds.
Bees collect pollen and nectar
from flowers to feed their larvae.
Nectar in a hive is made into
honey for winter food.

BEE-KEEPING
For thousands of years people have
kept bees for their honey. Modern
hives have racks of frames, each with a
ready-made comb of cells. Individual frames
can be removed and the honey drained.

POLLINATION
Other insects, such as butterflies, also
pollinate flowers. Many flowers are a
special color or shape to attract
particular insects. These insects
receive pollen and nectar in
the process of carrying pollen
to another flower.

+2

+6

POLLEN BASKETS

Bees carry pollen back to their nest in special pollen baskets on their back legs. The baskets are made from curved bristles. A bee uses its front legs to grab pollen from its furry body and put it in the baskets.

Shape of dance shows bees direction of flowers.

BEE COMMUNICATION

When a honeybee finds flowers with nectar it tells other bees in the hive by dancing. The bee conveys the distance of the flowers by how fast it shakes its abdomen, and the direction by the angle of its dance.

Pollen basket

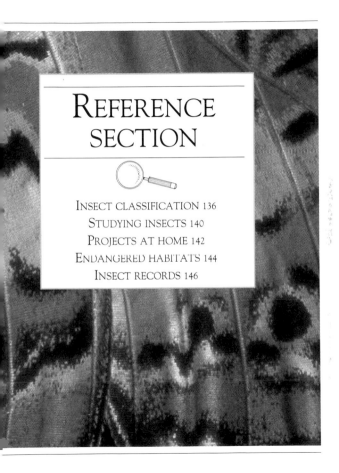

REFERENCE
SECTION

INSECT CLASSIFICATION

IN ORDER TO DISCUSS the different species of living things, we classify them into a series of categories according to the features they have in common. The largest category is the kingdom, which includes all animals. The kingdom is divided into smaller categories such as classes and orders, which are further divided until individual species are reached. The chart on pages 137-139 lists 24 insect orders and some of the features that define them.

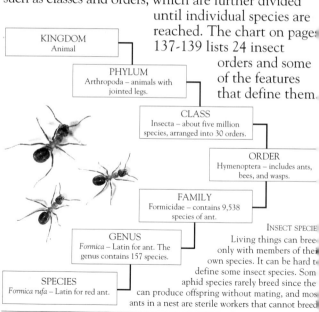

KINGDOM
Animal

PHYLUM
Arthropoda – animals with jointed legs.

CLASS
Insecta – about five million species, arranged into 30 orders.

ORDER
Hymenoptera – includes ants, bees, and wasps.

FAMILY
Formicidae – contains 9,538 species of ant.

GENUS
Formica – Latin for ant. The genus contains 157 species.

SPECIES
Formica rufa – Latin for red ant.

INSECT SPECIES
Living things can breed only with members of their own species. It can be hard to define some insect species. Some aphid species rarely breed since they can produce offspring without mating, and most ants in a nest are sterile workers that cannot breed

ORDER	SPECIES	CHARACTERISTICS
COLLEMBOLA	Springtails	Primitive wingless insects; often found on soil in vast numbers; incomplete metamorphosis
THYSANURA	Silverfish	Primitive wingless insects, sometimes scaly; found in caves and damp houses; incomplete metamorphosis
EPHEMEROPTERA	Mayflies	Soft-bodied and relatively delicate; larvae found in freshwater, adults have no feeding apparatus and live only a few days; incomplete metamorphosis
ODONATA	Dragonflies and damselflies	Generally large insects with big eyes; found worldwide; either carnivorous or herbivorous; larvae are predators in fresh water; incomplete metamorphosis
PLECOPTERA	Stoneflies	Adults are either herbivorous or do not feed at all and usually live along riverbanks; larvae live in freshwater; incomplete metamorphosis
BLATTODEA	Cockroaches	Omnivorous (eating both animals and plants) insects, often scavengers; flattened, oval body; found worldwide; incomplete metamorphosis
ISOPTERA	Termites, also known as white ants	Social, soft-bodied insects that live in vast colonies, each with one queen who lays all the eggs; most species feed on wood; incomplete metamorphosis
MANTODEA	Mantids	Predatory insects with large eyes, a mobile, triangular head, and grasping front legs; found mostly in the tropics; incomplete metamorphosis

ORDER	SPECIES	CHARACTERISTICS
DERMAPTERA	Earwigs	Omnivorous insects with fan-shaped hind wings, long antennae, and pincers on the tail; incomplete metamorphosis
ORTHOPTERA	Grasshoppers and crickets	Grass-feeding insects with large back legs modified for jumping; some species wingless; incomplete metamorphosis
PHASMATODEA	Leaf insects, stick insects	Leaf-feeding insects with camouflaged, flattened, or very slender bodies that resemble sticks or leaves; incomplete metamorphosis
PSOCOPTERA	Barklice and booklice	Small chewing insects that feed on tree bark, in packets of food, and in book bindings; often have short wings or none at all; incomplete metamorphosis
PHTHIRAPTERA	Parasitic lice	Parasites of birds and mammals, live on skin and feed on feathers, skin, or blood; wingless; incomplete metamorphosis
HEMIPTERA	Bugs	Insects with piercing and sucking mouthparts; feed on plants, insects, or mammals; incomplete metamorphosis
THYSANOPTERA	Thrips	Small or tiny insects with fringed wings; herbivorous with sucking mouthparts; some forms have short wings or none at all; incomplete metamorphosis
MEGALOPTERA	Alderflies, dobsonflies	Larvae are aquatic and carnivorous, adults have long, threadlike antennae; incomplete metamorphosis

ORDER	SPECIES	CHARACTERISTICS
NEUROPTERA	Lacewings, antlions	Predatory as larvae; adults are either carnivorous or herbivorous; incomplete metamorphosis
COLEOPTERA	Beetles	Very varied insects, with a front pair of wings modified into hard cases (elytra) covering the second pair; found worldwide; complete metamorphosis
MECOPTERA	Scorpionflies	Small predatory insects with biting mouthparts, found in woodlands; some forms short-winged or wingless; larvae are caterpillar-like; complete metamorphosis
SIPHONAPTERA	Fleas	Wingless insects with jumping hind legs; parasites of birds and mammals, feeding on blood with piercing and sucking mouthparts; complete metamorphosis
DIPTERA	True flies	Two-winged adults feed on plants and animals and in rotting vegetation; found worldwide in all habitats; larvae (maggots) are legless; complete metamorphosis
TRICHOPTERA	Caddisflies	Larvae live in fresh water and build a protective case around their body; adults either feed from flowers or do not feed at all; complete metamorphosis
LEPIDOPTERA	Butterflies and moths	Mouthparts form coiled proboscis; adults drink nectar, but in some species feed very little; larvae (caterpillars) eat mainly plants; complete metamorphosis
HYMENOPTERA	Wasps, ants, and bees	Mainly carnivorous insects, although some are herbivorous; some species live in highly ordered societies; females may have sting; complete metamorphosis

STUDYING INSECTS

ONE OF THE BEST ways to learn about an insect is to study it up close, either by observing the insect in its natural habitat or by capturing a specimen for a short time to examine it even more closely. Keep a record of when and where the insect was found, and its appearance, behavior, and habitat.

Gall

OAK LEAF WITH WASP GALLS

MAKE AN INSECT TRAP

Even a small garden may contain hundreds of different types of insect. Setting up a series of pitfall traps is a good way of catching several insects for a closer look. You will need a trowel, plastic cups, large stones, and flat, square pieces of wood.

TROWEL

STONES

CUPS

WOOD

1 Dig a hole for a cup. The top of the cup must be at ground level. Put one cup inside another. You can remove the inner cup to examine your catch.

2 Put cups in different places around the garden: under trees, on bare soil, among herbs, next to a pond, or in the middle of the lawn.

3 Place the wood on stones over each trap to form a protective cover. Inspect the traps regularly and record which insects you find.

R AND BRUSH

ost insects are small and move quickly. To get a
tter look at an insect, carefully use a paint
ush to knock one into a glass jar. Make
re to keep the insect cool, and after
amining it, let it go in the
me place it was caught.

*Pictures and
notes made with
pencils won't run
if it rains.*

*Make holes in
the lid of the jar
so the insects
can breathe.*

PAD AND PENCILS

Keep a notebook to record the
insects you discover. Make
drawings of the insects to show
size and color, and record
information about the habitat
in which they were found.

*Make additional
drawings of any
special features an
insect may have.*

MAGNIFYING GLASS

When studying insects, one
essential piece of equipment is a
magnifying glass. A simple hand
lens that magnifies ten times
will clearly reveal details barely
visible with the naked eye.

*A magnifying
glass will show features
such as compound eyes
in much greater detail.*

PROJECTS AT HOME

A CATERPILLAR
is an ideal
subject for
observing an
insect's life cycle. In
captivity, it will grow,
pupate, and finally emerge as
an adult. Keep a community of pond
insects in an aquarium to study the way
they live – both above and below the
surface of the water.

*Caterpillars are
soft so they should
handled gently.
Avoid handling
caterpillars with ha
– these may sting
and cause a rash.*

CATERPILLAR BOX
When you have found a caterpillar, put it
in a box with plenty of leaves from its
feeding plant. Keep the box clean and dry
and replace the leaves as they are eaten
or begin to shrivel. After the caterpillar
pupates and becomes a butterfly or moth,
release it in the place the caterpillar was found.

INSECTS AND SAUCERS
Use three saucers of food
to see how different food
scents attract different
insects. Place fruit in
one saucer, gravy in
another, and water in the
third. Use white and yellow
saucers for the water, to see
if color draws insects.

*Butterflies and
wasps are drawn
to feed on the
sugary fruit.*

*The smell of the
meat in the
gravy will
attract insect
carnivores.*

*Clean water has
no smell – but a
colored plate may
draw insects.*

OW TO MAKE YOUR OWN SECT AQUARIUM

t up an aquarium to observe nd insects in a habitat like eir own. You will need a astic aquarium, some gravel, ew large stones, some dead cks, and a few water plants.

YOU WILL NEED

STICKS

GRAVEL

LARGE STONES   WATER PLANTS

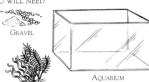

AQUARIUM

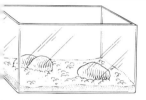

1 Cover the bottom of the aquarium with about 2 in (5 cm) gravel and scatter the large stones round. The gravel will provide a ome for microscopic animals that ill help to keep the water clean.

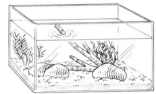

2 Fill the aquarium by pouring water over an upside-down bowl. In this way you do not disturb the gravel. Next root the water plants into the gravel and put in the sticks so that they poke out above the water.

3 Using a pond net, catch some insects nd snails from a local ond, place them in ur aquarium, and atch what they do. ou can buy live aterfleas in a petshop. hey help keep the ater clean and provide good source of food for e predators.

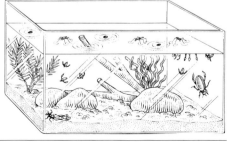

ENDANGERED HABITATS

ALL OVER THE WORLD the natural environment is
shrinking as people exploit and destroy natural
habitats. The threats come from agriculture, forestry,
mining, road building, the spread of towns, and
pollution. Even nature reserves can have problems
with increasing numbers of visitors. As habitats
disappear, so do the communities of plants, insects,
and other animals that live there.

HABITAT	REASONS FOR DESTRUCTION	INSECT EXAMPLES
RAINFOREST	Species-rich forests felled for timber or replaced by grasslands for cattle or crops. These support few insect species and are plagued by pests because the natural predators have gone.	Hercules beetle; Queen Alexandra's birdwing butterfly; 8-spotted skipper butterfly; Wallace's giant bee
FOREST	Large trees in forests felled for timber. Access roads in forest encourage farmers to settle who then clear more trees. Some trees and the insects associated with them threatened with extinction.	Periodical cicada; Giant carrion beetle; Sugarfoot moth fly; European wood ant; Frigate island giant tenebrionid beetle
SEMIDESERT AREAS	Domestic livestock over-grazing leads to erosion of topsoil. Heat quickly evaporates irrigation water, resulting in salts building up in soil. Fewer plants can grow leading to expansion of deserts.	St. Helena earwig; Belkin's dune tabanid fly; Avalon hairstreak butterfly; Ravoux's slavemaker ant

HABITAT	REASONS FOR DESTRUCTION	INSECT EXAMPLES
TROPICAL DRY FOREST AREAS	Leaves fall off trees in dry season. Trees are destroyed by burning to produce grasslands for cattle. Fires are allowed to burn out of control. One of the most threatened habitats.	Giant wetas; Small hemiphlebia damselfly; Lord Howe Island stick insect; Australian nothomyrmecia ant
PRAIRIES	Natural grasslands rich in wild flowers and insect species are plowed and treated with fertilizers and insecticides to produce cereal crops and "improved" grasslands for cattle.	Delta green ground beetle; Dakota skipper; Wiest's sphinx moth
LAKES AND RIVERS	Water is polluted by fertilizers running off fields. Pollution from sewage and industrial waste, and metal pollution from mine wastes. River channels are straightened and dredged.	Large blue lake mayfly; Freya's damselfly; Relict Himalayan dragonfly; Florida spiketail dragonfly; Tobias caddis fly
GRASSLANDS	Drainage of water meadows and plowing of grasslands for crops destroys natural plants. Addition of fertilizers results in domination by aggressive species of grass with fewer wild flowers and insects.	Pygmy hog sucking louse; Large blue butterfly; Bay checkerspot butterfly
BOGS AND PEATLANDS	Land is drained for agriculture, such as planting of timber trees for commercial forestry. Cutting and extraction of peat for use in gardens or as fuel for power stations.	Ohio emerald dragonfly; Flumiense swallowtail butterfly; Harris' mimic swallowtail butterfly

INSECT RECORDS

INSECTS ARE the most numerous animals on Earth. Their success is mostly due to their small size and remarkable adaptability. The following are some of the more amazing insect record-breakers.

SIZE

- Bulkiest insect: goliath beetle – 4⅓ in (110 mm) long weighing 3½ oz (100 g)

- Smallest: mymarid wasp – 0.0067 in (17 mm) long

- Largest wingspan: *Thysania agrippina* moth – 11 in (28 cm) wide

- Largest water insect: giant water bug from Venezuela and Brazil – 4½ in (11.5 cm) long

- Most numerous insect: springtails – about 540,000 per sq ft (50,000 per sq m) in grassland

FLIGHT

- Fastest ever: a giant prehistoric dragonfly probably had to fly at least 43 mph (69 km/h) to stay airborne

- Fastest-flying living insects: hawk-moths – reach top speed of 33⅓ mph (53.6 km/h)

- Fastest wingbeat: the midge *Forcipomyia* – 62,760 beats per minute

- Slowest wingbeat: swallowtail butterfly – 300 beats per minute

- Farthest migration: painted lady butterfly – 4,000 miles (6,436 km) from North Africa to Iceland

PESTS

- Most fatalities: more than half of all deaths since the Stone Age are due to malaria-carrying mosquitoes. Rat fleas carry a plague which killed 20 million people in 14th-century Europe

- Most poisonous: about 40,000 people are killed each year by wasp or bee stings

- Most disease-ridden: the housefly transmits more than 30 diseases and parasites

- Most destructive: a locust swarm can eat 20,000 tons (tonnes) of crops per day

NESTS

• Largest: Australian termite nests – up to 23 ft (7 m) high and 100 ft (31 m) in diameter at the base

• Tallest: nests of African termite – 42 ft (12.8 m) high

• Deepest: nests of desert termite – 131 ft (40 m) below ground

COMMUNICATION

• Loudest: cicada – its song can be heard by humans from a distance of ¼ mile (400 m)

• Most sensitive sense of smell: Indian moon moth – can detect pheromones of a mate from a distance of over 6¾ miles (11 km)

LEGS/ANTENNAE

• Longest: giant stick insect – 20 in (51 cm)

• Longest antennae: New guinea longhorn beetle – 7½ in (20 cm)

• Longest jump: Desert locust – 19½ in (50 cm), which is 10 times its own body length

TOUGHEST

• Larvae of ephyrid flies live in the waters of hot springs at 140° F (60°C)

• The snow flea remains active at temperatures of 5° F (-15°C)

• Larvae of the midge Polypedilum can survive years without water and three days in liquid nitrogen (-321°F, -196°C)

LIFESTYLE

• Longest lifecycle: periodic cicada – 17 years

• Longest-lived larva: a wood-boring beetle larva once survived for 45 years

• Shortest-lived insect: fruitfly – can complete its entire lifecycle in less than 14 days

EGGS

• Largest: ⅖ in x ⅙₀ in (10.2 mm x 4.2 mm) laid by cerambycid beetle, Titanus giganteus

• Longest time in the egg stage: 9½ months by the cerambycid beetle Saperda carcharia

• Most eggs laid: the queen Macrotermes termite can lay 40,000 eggs per day

Resources

UNITED STATES

PLACES WITH INSECT
COLLECTIONS TO VISIT:

**American Museum of
Natural History**
Central Park West
at 79th Street
New York, NY 10024

**Buffalo Museum of
Science**
1020 Humboldt
Parkway,
Buffalo, NY 14211

Butterfly World
3600 West Sample
Road
Coconut Creek,
FL 33073

**The Carnegie Museum
of Natural History**
4400 Forbes Avenue
Pittsburgh, PA 15213

**The Denver Museum
of Natural History**
2001 Colorado Blvd.
Denver, CO 80205

**Field Museum of
Natural History**
1400 South Lakeshore
Drive
Chicago, IL 60605

**Houston Museum of
Natural Science**
1 Hermann Circle
Drive
Houston, TX 77030

Liberty Science Center
Liberty State Park
251 Philip Street
Jersey City, NJ 07305

**Natural History
Museum of Los
Angeles County**
900 Exposition Blvd.
Los Angeles,
CA 90007

**The National Museum
of Natural History**
Smithsonian
Institution
Dept. of Entomology
Attn: Collections Mgr
Mail Stop #: NHB 16
Constitution Ave.
and 10th Street, NW
Washington,
DC 20560

**The Schiele Museum
of Natural History &
Planetarium, Inc.**
1500 East Garrison
Blvd.
Gastonia, NC 28054

SOCIETIES TO JOIN:

**Entomological Society
of America**
9301 Annapolis Road
Lanham, MD 20706

**The Lepidopterists'
Society**
c/o Kelly M. Richers
9417 Carvalho Court
Bakersfield, CA 93311

assachusetts
atterfly Club
 Madeline
hampagne
ond Avenue
xboro, MA 02035

ew York
ntomological Society
 American Museum
 Natural History
ntral Park West
79th Street
ew York, NY 10024

orth American
atterfly Association
 Delaware Road
orristown, NJ 07960

he Young
ntomologists' Society
 07 W. Grand River
venue
ansing, MI 48906

CANADA

Biological Survey of Canada
(Terrestrial Arthropods)
Canadian Museum
of Nature
P.O. Box 3443
Station D, Ottawa,
Ontario, R1P 6P4

The Manitoba Museum
Winnipeg MB R3B 0N2

Nova Scotia Museum of Natural History
1747 Summer Street
Halifax NS B3H 3A6

The Royal British Columbia Museum
675 Bellville Street
Victoria, BC V8W 9W2

Royal Ontario Museum
Dept. of Entomology
100 Queens Park
Toronto ON M5S 2C6

Spencer Entomological Museum
University of British
Columbia
Dept. of Zoology
Vancouver BC
V6T 1W5

SOCIETIES TO JOIN:

Entomological Society of Canada
393 Winston Avenue
Ottawa ON K2A 1Y8

Entomological Society of Quebec
Insectarium du
Montréal
4581 Sherbrooke Est
Montréal QC H1X 2B2

Toronto Entomologists' Association
c/o 34 Seaton Drive
Aurora ON L4G 2K1

Glossary

ABDOMEN
Segmented section of arthropod's body behind thorax which contains the digestive and reproductive organs.

ANTENNAE
Two appendages on the head of insects and other arthropods used mainly for touching and smelling.

ARTHROPOD
An invertebrate with jointed appendages and a hardened exoskeleton.

BROOD CELL
A space or structure in a bee or wasp nest where a single egg is laid and the larva develops until it becomes an adult.

CAMOUFLAGE
The means of disguising the body in order to go unnoticed by predators or prey.

CARNIVOROUS
Flesh-eating.

CASTE
In social insect societies, a group containing individuals which

perform specialized tasks, such as "workers" in wasp nests or "soldiers" in ant nests.

CATERPILLAR
Any wormlike insect larva, but usually refers to the larva of moths and butterflies.

CERCI
Two spine-shaped sensory growths at the end of the abdomen of some arthropods.

CHRYSALIS
The pupa of a moth or butterfly.

CLASPERS
Two pincerlike appendages on the abdomen of male insects which grasp the female during mating.

COCOON
Protective silk casing which the larvae of many insects weave around themselves prior to pupation.

COLONY
A group of social insects living and working together and sharing a nest.

COMPLETE METAMORPHOSIS
The type of development from egg to adult in which there are distinct stages including a pupal stage; usually the larva looks very different from the adult and also has a different diet.

COMPOUND EYE
An eye composed of many separate eyes called ommatidia. Each ommatidium is capable of vision.

COURTSHIP DANCE
Dancelike movements, often performed in flight, between two insects before matin

DISRUPTIVE COLORATION
A combination of colors and patterns on the body which disrupt its shape, making it hard to recognize.

ELYTRA
The front wings of beetles which are hardened and protect the body.

ENTOMOLOGY
The scientific study of insects.

EXOSKELETON
The external skeleton of an arthropod.

EYESPOTS
Markings on an insect's body which look like eyes for frightening or distracting predators.

FOSSIL
The remains of something that once lived, preserved as stone.

FUNGUS
A simple plant, usually growing on other plants and animals and often causing decay and disease.

FUNGUS GARDEN
Fungus cultivated in a nest as food by leaf-cutter ants and certain species of termite.

GALL
An abnormal growth on a plant caused by the presence of an insect's egg or its feeding activities.

GILLS
Outgrowths on an aquatic insect's body by which the insect breathes underwater.

GRUB
An insect larva, especially of beetles, which lives underground or in rotting wood.

HALTERES
The hind wings of flies (Diptera) which have been modified into clubbed stalks and are used as balancers in flight.

HERBIVOROUS
Plant-eating.

HONEYDEW
A sweet, sticky liquid secreted by aphids and treehoppers, derived from the sap of plants on which they feed.

HONEY GUIDES
Lines on the flower petals of certain plants which reflect ultraviolet light and direct insects to the pollen and nectar.

HOST
Animal or plant on which a parasite or herbivore feeds and lays its eggs.

INCOMPLETE METAMORPHOSIS
The type of development of insects in which the nymphs hatch looking like small versions of the adults and there is no pupal stage.

INVERTEBRATE
An animal without a backbone.

LARVA
The stage in an insect's life between egg and pupa. The young stage of insects that do not pupate is called a nymph.

LEAF MINERS
Insects which live and feed inside a leaf, creating a mine, or tunnel, as they feed.

MAMMAL
A warm-blooded animal which drinks its mother's milk when it is young.

MATING
The reproductive act between a male and female of the same species where the male puts sperm in the female in order to create young.

METAMORPHOSIS
The process of insect growth from egg to adult by which the body shape metamorphoses, or changes, as it grows.

MIMICRY
The process whereby one insect species copies the coloration and behavior of another species, usually for the purpose of protection from predators.

MOLTING
The shedding of old skin to be replaced by a new skin.

MUD PUDDLING
The habit of butterflies, usually in the tropics, of gathering in groups to drink from muddy puddles in order to obtain essential minerals and salts.

NECTAR
A sugary fluid found in flowers.

NOCTURNAL
Being active by night and resting by day.

NYMPH
See LARVA.

OCELLI
Simple eyes which have a limited function, probably only detecting light and shade.

OMMATIDIUM
A single part of a compound eye capable of detailed vision.

OMNIVOROUS
Having a diet of both animal and plant food.

OVIPOSITOR
The egg-laying tube of insects.

PARASITE
An animal which completes its development on, or in, the body of another animal without benefiting its host in any way.

PALPS
Sensory organs beside the jaws of some insects.

PHEROMONES
Chemicals produced by insects of both sexes which act as a sexual attractant to members of the opposite sex.

POLLEN
A flower's male sex cells which fertilize the female sex cell (ovule).

POLLINATION
The process by which the pollen of one flower is transported, usually by insects or by the wind, to the female part (ovary) of another plant of the same species to produce seeds.

PREDATOR
An animal which hunts other animals for food.

PROBOSCIS
The long, flexible feeding organ of insects such as butterflies and moths, which is used for sucking up liquids.

PROLEGS (FALSE LEGS)
Fleshy growths on the abdomen of some insect larvae, especially caterpillars, which function as legs.

PUPA, PUPAL STAGE
The inactive, non-feeding stage of insects which undergo complete metamorphosis, when the larva transforms into an adult.

ROSTRUM
The piercing and sucking, beaklike mouthparts of true bugs.

SALIVA
A liquid secreted in to the mouth which begins the process of digesting food. In some insects the saliva is deadly and is injected into prey, killing the prey and dissolving its insides.

SCALES
Modified hairs which have become flattened, especially found in butterflies and moths.

SIMPLE EYE
See OCELLI.

SOCIAL
Living in groups.

SOLDIER
A caste member from a termite or ant colony which has an enlarged head and jaws used in a defensive role to protect the other members of the nest.

SPECIES
A group of animals or plants which can breed only with each other and produce fertile offspring.

SPERM
A male cell which is put inside a female during mating to join with her eggcell, which creates a new individual.

SPIRACLES
External openings of the tracheae on the body of an insect through which the insect breathes.

SPITTLE
Frothy liquid produced by certain plant bugs

in which they hide from predators and which stops them from dehydrating.

STING
The modified ovipositor of certain wasps, bees, and ants, which has lost its egg-laying function and is used to inject venom into prey or enemies.

SWARMING
Any huge group of insects traveling together, but usually the behavior of honeybees when the queen and a large number of workers leave their nest to set up a new nest elsewhere.

TARSUS
The insect's "foot," consisting of between one and five segments and one or two claws for gripping surfaces.

TEMPERATE REGIONS
Parts of the Earth between the tropical and the polar regions, with moderate temperatures.

THORAX
The part of an arthropod's body between the head and abdomen that bears the legs and wings.

TRACHEAE
Tubes in the body of an insect which transport oxygen.

TROPICAL REGIONS
Parts of the Earth around the equator with hot temperatures all year.

ULTRAVIOLET
Beyond the violet end of the light spectrum, ultraviolet is invisible to most mammals, but visible to most insects.

VENOM
A poison which is often deadly, produced by many predatory insects for injecting into prey or enemies.

WARNING COLORATION
Bright, conspicuous body coloring used by many insects with weapons or poisonous bodies; predators learn to avoid these insects.

WORKER
A member of an insect colony which is sterile (cannot breed) and whose duties include caring for the larvae, maintaining the nest, and foraging for food.

Latin name index

Lantern bug (*Fulgora aeternaria*)

Large blue butterfly (*Maculinea arion*)

Large copper butterfly (*Lycaena dispar*)

Large white (cabbage white) butterfly (*Pieris brassicae*)

Macleay's specter (*Extatosoma tiaratum*)

Marble gall wasp (*Andricus kollari*)

Marbled white butterfly (*Melanargia galathea*)

Merveille du jour moth (*Dichnonia aprilina*)

Mexican bean beetle (*Epilachna varivestis*)

Mole cricket (*Gryllotalpa gryllotalpa*)

Monarch butterfly (*Danaus plexippus*)

Namib Desert beetle (*Onymacris unguicularis*)

Nut weevil (*Curculio glandium*)

Oak bush cricket (*Meconema thalassinum*)

Oak silkmoth (*Antheraea harti*)

Parent bug (*Elasmucha grisea*)

Parasol ant (*Atta cephalotes*)

Peacock butterfly (*Inachis io*)

Pond skater (*Gerris gibbifer*)

Postman butterfly (*Heliconius melpomene*)

Purple emperor (*Apatura iris*)

Puss moth (*Cerura vinula*)

Saddle-back moth (*Sibine stimulea*)

Silver-spotted skipper butterfly (*Epargyreus clarus*)

Silver-striped hawk moth (*Hippotion celerio*)

Silver-washed fratillary butterfly (*Argynnis paphia*)

Small postman butterfly (*Heliconius erato*)

Snakefly (*Raphidia notata*)

Soldier beetle (*Rhagonycha fulva*)

South American dung beetle (*Coprophanaeus lancifer*)

Speckled bush cricket (*Leptophyes punctatissima*)

Speckled wood butterfly (*Pararge aegeria*)

Springtail (*Isotoma palustris*)

Spurge hawk moth (*Hyles euphorbiae*)

Stag beetle (*Lucanus cervus*)

Stonefly (*Diura bipunctata*)

Striped blue crow butterfly (*Euploea mulciber*)

Striped-winged grasshopper (*Stenobothrus lineatus*)

Surinam cockroach (*Pycnoscelis surinamensis*)

Tarantula hawk wasp (*Pepsis heros*)

Tiger beetle (*Cicindela campestris*)

Vaporer moth (*Orgyia antiqua*)

Water boatman (*Notonecta glauca*)

Water measurer (*Hydrometra stagnorum*)

Water scorpion (*Nepa cinerea*)

Weevil-hunting wasp (*Cerceris arenaria*)

West African termites (*Macrotermes bellicosus*)

Whirligig beetle (*Dineutes politus*)

Wood ant (*Formica rufa*)

Wood cricket (*Nemobius sylvestris*)

Index